I'M JUST HERE FOR DESSERT

*To my husband, Nick, the love of my life. Thank you for
believing in, supporting, nurturing and encouraging me.
And to my kids, for giving me spirit, endless hugs and kisses,
and the time to breathe life into this book.*

I'M JUST HERE FOR DESSERT

macarons, mini cakes, ice creams, waffles & more

CAROLINE KHOO *of* NECTAR AND STONE

MURDOCH BOOKS

SYDNEY · LONDON

CONTENTS

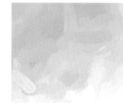

Navigating this book

Like a cake, this book has been designed and constructed in layers. Within each layer, you'll find tips and step-by-step instructions to help you master key techniques and recipes. You'll also find little nods of inspiration to help you build your design skills as you go.

I'll share some great base recipes you can count on, as well as plenty of pretty and simple tips for turning those desserts into something truly memorable — things that spark joy and create moments that will be treasured by your friends and family.

Each new skill you acquire can be applied to the following layers, and to completely new things as you branch out from these recipes and ideas to create designs that reflect your own unique story.

WE ARE EATING CAKE FOR YOU TODAY

*The only limitation in dessert design is
how far you are prepared to go.*

My Journey

I DECIDED TO TRAVEL ALONE ...

TO EXPERIENCE THE WORLD,
CONFRONT MY OWN SILENCE,
DISCOVER THINGS AND
BUILD THROUGH MY OWN EYES.
WHEN I DID THIS, I BEGAN
TO FEEL THE FREEDOM
IN EXPLORING, LEARNING,
CREATING AND DESIGNING.

Nectar and Stone

NEVER IN MY WILDEST DREAMS did I imagine I would write a dessert design and recipe book. It is truly an honour to be able to share my journey, creativity, knowledge, energy and the many lessons I've learned through trial and error with you.

Even though this career came as somewhat of a surprise to me, food has always been a central part of my life. As a child, I enjoyed being in the kitchen with my mother and learning the Greek recipes she had been taught as a young girl. I never expected those experiences to form the foundations of a new career, but they did.

My Greek background has now fused with my husband's Asian background, and the result is a rich and beautiful blend of traditions and flavours. His culture is very family-focused, as is mine, and this has really instilled in me a feeling of unity and enjoyment when it comes to how I perceive food, and desserts.

My work/life history is a blend of fashion, politics and medicine, and I believe each of these areas has played an integral role in leading me to this place. My political and medical experience taught me how to connect with people and understand their needs — a fundamental skill I needed to build relationships with customers and sell my products. But it is the time I spent in the fashion industry that has helped me create the platform from which I began shaping a feminine aesthetic — one that would grow into a very distinct signature style.

When I became a mother to two boys, my home was transformed into a boyish world, and I found myself drawing on that feminine style from my time in the fashion industry in order to carve out my own identity. Along with the joys of motherhood came the challenges of feeding my toddlers. Finding creative ways to interest them in food became an obsession, and I soon discovered that I was most successful when I helped them eat with their eyes first. This feminine aesthetic of mine came to the rescue once again, as I'd entice them to eat by making their food look beautiful.

It was after I had my second child that my obsession with desserts announced itself as more than a hobby. The energy I'd been putting into making food look beautiful started to channel itself into the desserts I was baking for my friends and family. The people around me noticed something unique and special in what I was doing, and they encouraged me to explore it.

So, after a lot of research, planning and learning, I started my dessert business, Nectar and Stone. I'll admit I was very scared about failure — starting something from nothing really terrified me. But, at the same time, my creative energy was in overdrive and I needed to pour it into something I could share. Something in me told me to pursue it and give it a go.

I gave myself one year ...

she designed a life that would
always involve flowers

Being open and confronting fear

STARTING MY OWN BUSINESS is one of the scariest things I've ever done, but sometimes we need to face our fears and challenge ourselves in order to build, grow and learn. I'm sharing this aspect of my story with you because it might be a part of your journey, too. Perhaps there is something you need to embrace in order to succeed in your own business or to tackle a dream that seems too difficult to approach.

When I decided to turn my hobby into a business, I made a commitment to start from the very beginning. I did this by revisiting the basic recipes and techniques I planned on using for my new business. By testing and retesting recipes, and practising techniques until I was completely happy with the results, I was able to master these areas of my business completely before progressing to the next step of the plan. I approached things this way because I needed to be confident that I had solid foundations I could count on in order to create consistent results once things were up and running.

Desserts tell a story: they can take the person eating them on a sensory journey from the first look to the last bite. It was important to me that my creations reveal layers and complexity, even in their simplicity. So once I'd mastered the foundations, I worked on developing my signature style until I was creating desserts that were beautiful and simple, yet also sophisticated. I infused meaning into my designs by taking inspiration from the things I loved and things I saw around me. As I broke

I believe that our past experiences are the driving forces

behind
our future ones.

larger challenges into smaller ones, and perfected one thing at a time before moving on to the next, I found that my confidence grew, and the process of creating desserts and building a business became more manageable and enjoyable.

By repeating a similar process in this book, I hope to provide you with the skills and tools you'll need to shape your personal style of dessert design. So this is where we'll start our journey together: mastering the basics and building from there.

@nectarandstone

SHOOTING MY DESSERTS AT HOME and sharing them on social media allowed me to connect with creative people working in many different industries and countries. It also provided a platform for my photography to be seen, my dessert designs to be celebrated and for traditional styles of dessert presentation and techniques to be challenged in a fun and inclusive way.

It has been humbling to have an amazing worldwide community support me on Instagram. The people who follow @nectarandstone have been travelling with me on my journey since 2013. They've watched me grow, change and refine my skills along the way. I'll be forever thankful to them for believing in me and advocating for my work.

Because putting images of my work on social media has been such a big part of my success, I've included a few of my favourite tips for capturing and sharing your own triumphs on page 40. Hopefully, these will be useful to you, whether you plan on starting your own business and publicising it on social media or you just want to take some great shots for your own pleasure.

Perfection comes from mastering simplicity

Foundations

THE BASICS

Start at the very beginning

Perfection comes from mastering simplicity and building from there.

UNDERSTANDING, LEARNING AND MASTERING the basics when it comes to baking and decorating techniques are the essential building blocks of dessert design. When I talk about 'basics', I don't just mean basic techniques and principles. 'Basics' also refers to equipment and, of course, recipes.

There are many beautiful recipes in this book, but they are, for the most part, 'basic' in the sense that the ingredients and flavours are simple and classic. Sharing elaborate or complicated recipes is not the purpose of this book — there are plenty of those available in the public domain — rather, it's to help you perfect a few basic (but delicious) recipes and master some fundamental techniques. Once you have these in your tool belt, you'll be able to apply them to so many styles of dessert. This will allow you to be resourceful when it may seem like nothing can be made.

Though my recipes are simple, I place a strong emphasis on using quality ingredients and the right tools, and on allowing an adequate amount of time to do even the quickest of steps properly. By keeping things simple and dedicating yourself to completing each and every stage methodically, you'll be able to focus on refining your technique and building solid foundations on which to start work on the decorating side of dessert design.

Working with colour is another aspect of dessert design that falls under the umbrella of 'basics' in my mind. This is because working with colour confidently is a crucial part of creating something that is striking, sophisticated and pleasing to the eye. Forming a solid understanding of how colours work together will allow you to add and build layers to your designs.

But past all of this lies my true goal: to help you develop your creative instincts. I want to encourage you to see inspiration everywhere and then translate that into something beautiful and unexpected — something all your own. To me, this is far more valuable than having you faithfully recreate my recipes and designs.

Finding your own style, that is the true journey.

Risk taker

I had a deep desire
to stand out from the crowd.

OVER TIME, I'VE TRIALLED MANY TOOLS and pieces of equipment. My personal style only manifested itself once I found the techniques I liked the most and the tools best suited to creating them. Because of this, I think that experimenting with the tools that you have, and with any new tools you buy, is a really good habit to get into. A round cookie cutter, for example, can also be used as a stencil for meringue wreaths, to cut out circles of fondant for cake decorating, or to trace circles on cakes to be filled in by icing. Only by experimenting can you discover the full range of things your tools are capable of. It is okay to break some rules, so enjoy yourself and take a few risks.

When I first started using piping (icing) tools on my cupcakes, I tested out many pipe tips to find out how the frosting looked when piped at different angles, rotations and levels of pressure. Once I felt I'd mastered a particular tip, I'd move on to the next one. And when it came to decorating my cupcakes, I didn't like limiting myself to using just one pipe tip per cupcake, so I created cupcake designs that involved two pipe tips and two different colours of frosting.

I urge you to think outside the box when it comes to finding your tools. Art supply shops are great places to browse for different brushes and palette knives, which can be great for cake decorating. If you see something and it sparks an idea, try it. Don't rule equipment out just because it's not in the baking aisle of a kitchen shop.

There are
no limitations to
what you can use
for decorating.
There are so many
objects that can be
used to design and
create — be open
and think outside
the cake store.

Sometimes the tools would guide her decorating

Harnessing inspiration

VENTURE OUT TO EXPERIENCE YOUR EVERYDAY SURROUNDINGS WITH NEW EYES. TRY DOING THIS EACH DAY, EVEN IF ONLY FOR A FEW MINUTES. I MAKE IT A MORNING RITUAL TO STEP OUTSIDE AND SEE THE SKY. WHATEVER YOU CHOOSE TO DO, MAKE IT ENJOYABLE AND FUN.

LOCAL FLORISTS

Become familiar with the different flowers available across the seasons. Let their shapes, colours, lengths, and the texture of their petals and leaves spark ideas. Be curious about new varieties of blooms. Buy a bunch and arrange them in a vase, then observe what they do over the week and watch how they appear in different lights.

ART SHOPS

A great art supply shop will provide plenty of inspiration as well as materials if you want to experiment with decorating, or work on an unrelated creative project (I find doing this often inspires new ideas). I like to paint with acrylics and watercolours, and find they're the perfect mediums for gaining new perspective on colour.

CAMERA IN HAND

Going out and taking pictures of the things you see can help you collect ideas and build concepts. I often take a stroll through my neighbourhood and take pictures of flowers growing in gardens, trees against pink skies and different rooftops.

HOME DÉCOR STORES

These stores have a variety of tableware and serveware that can be used to style desserts. They're also good places to see which colours, patterns and looks are trending. I tend to buy spoons and small serving plates in a few colours. Visit your local charity shop as well; they often have fantastic bargains and unique pieces.

CITY STROLLING

Venture into your nearest city and rediscover it by losing yourself and seeing it with new eyes. Observe the colours and shapes of the buildings, take notice of fashions in the stores and what people are wearing. These things can all lead to design concepts that can be developed and applied to dessert work.

BOOKSTORES

One of my favourite things to do is visit bookstores and add to my collection. I always browse the travel, garden and fashion sections. New ideas can be found in so many places; you just need to have an open mind and be observant.

Concept building

CONCEPT BUILDING IS AN IMPORTANT PART of my creative process, and it's a process that pops up in this book several times. I believe it's the key to making something truly unique, because the things I see and experience in my own life inform my ideas and become the concepts behind the finished designs, each of which has its own story.

For me, concept building always starts with getting outside and looking around. After exploring your local surroundings, you may discover something you like and connect with. For example, on a walk in the city one day I spotted a beautiful white building that was wonderfully stark in its simplicity. I also bought a bunch of poinsettias from my local nursery in a particularly striking shade of pink. Once I got home, these two images swirled around and married in my mind.

Elements of these two objects became the starting point for a cake design concept. The minimal silhouette and colour of the building provided the inspiration for the white frosted cake with clean lines and evenly applied colour. The arresting pink shade of the poinsettia leaves, along with their intricate pattern, provided the colour and detail for the finishing touches.

In sharing a few examples of my concept-building process, and showing you how everyday objects like a flower or an iron fence can be used as a jumping-off point for creating something completely unrelated (like a macaron), I hope you'll feel encouraged to try building your own concepts. Then the desserts you make will be a reflection of your unique perspective. Like anything else in life, the more you practise this process, the easier it becomes — and the more rewarding the results.

Working with colour

COLOUR PLAYS SUCH AN IMPORTANT ROLE in the design of a dessert. Not only does it set the tone and potential theme for the dessert (or the dessert table), it can also highlight other elements at a party, such as balloons, streamers, lighting or candles (if they are part of the look). Flowers, invitations and other props can also tie in beautifully with the desserts on display. For a wedding, you can even go so far as to match the tones of the cake or dessert with the colour of the bridesmaid dresses ... The possibilities are endless!

One of my favourite ways to design is to use a few shades of one colour — I love the look of different tones and highlights in a dessert. Generally, if I'm working with only one colour, I aim to incorporate three different shades of that colour in total. I may or may not add a contrasting colour to the dessert, it really depends on what type of look I want, what sort of mood I want to evoke, and the style, shape and theme of the dessert. All of these things need careful consideration when selecting which colours to work with. It's always good to do a quick sketch of what you imagine the finished dessert will look like before you start baking. Add some colour to the image so you can get an idea of how it might come together in real life.

Colour play

A simple (and cheap) way of finding colours that speak to you is to visit your local hardware or paint store. Browse their colour swatches, pick out the ones you like, then start mixing and matching to see what works well together. Take your favourite swatches home and use them as a visual guide when adding food colouring to buttercreams, cake batters and meringues. This will help you achieve the exact hues and tones you're after.

I also suggest creating a mood board of textures, colours and natural elements. Add things such as leaves and flowers when you find them, and let these guide you when designing and decorating.

Contrast

When identifying colours that go well together, it's important to consider the overall effect you're aiming to achieve. Using colour palettes is a good way to see if colours work together. For example, a pale pink might be used with a mustard yellow. Unconventional? Perhaps, but the right tones can contrast and work well together. Mix and match to find combinations that please your eye, then use those colours confidently in your designs.

Get organised, get ahead

THE IMPORTANCE OF PLANNING AND BEING ORGANISED BEFORE YOU BEGIN TACKLING A DESSERT CANNOT BE OVERSTATED. If you're making something special for an event, start thinking about the cake or dessert a couple of weeks beforehand to ensure you give yourself enough time to complete every stage properly. This might sound dramatic, but it is crucial to the success of your dessert. So make a checklist and plan your attack.

- Read the recipe over carefully.

- Purchase your ingredients.

- Get the props for styling and displaying together.

- Plan which days you'll be making each element and allow yourself more time than you think you'll need.

- Check your equipment to make sure everything is clean and in working order.

Once you've done these things, it's time to get started. For me, a big part of working efficiently and productively in the kitchen is having my workspace clean and organised, with things that make me happy in my line of sight. Get to know yourself in the kitchen and start each dessert journey by setting up your workspace exactly the way you want it.

MY WORKSPACE LIKES

LESS IS MORE

CLEAN AND TIDY

FRESH, GOOD-QUALITY INGREDIENTS

GOOD LIGHTING

MOOD BOARD FOR INSPIRATION

FRESH FLOWERS

CARED-FOR EQUIPMENT

CAMERA NEARBY

Key ingredients

THE QUALITY OF THE INGREDIENTS YOU USE HAS A DIRECT AND DRAMATIC IMPACT ON THE SUCCESS OF YOUR DESSERTS. BEFORE WE START, I WANT TO HIGHLIGHT A FEW INGREDIENTS YOU'LL BE WORKING WITH THROUGHOUT THE BOOK, AND EXPLAIN HOW AND WHY I LIKE TO USE THEM.

Eggs

I've always found eggs to be curious things. They're a simple, staple ingredient, yet they have a vast array of functions and uses. The more my baking skills progressed, the more I began to understand their importance. They can literally make or break your dessert.

Once I understood this, I paused and reflected on my baking. I realised that I needed to take a few steps back and work on how I was using a few key ingredients, eggs being one of them. I wanted to understand the science going on behind my baking, so this meant I produced many trial desserts before I was able to achieve consistently excellent results. This was especially true for desserts that called for egg whites.

After a lot of testing, I came to the conclusion that my meringues and macarons worked best when I used eggs that were less fresh than those used for cakes and cupcakes. Throughout this book, we'll explore using eggs as a whole, as a yolk and as a white. Working with them in their various forms will teach you how they behave in different situations.

I use 62 g (2.2 oz) free-range eggs (these are classified as extra-large eggs in Australia, but this may be different depending on where you live). I prefer to buy free-range eggs because I believe they are a better-quality ingredient than caged eggs, and that they yield the best results. If you have the opportunity, I strongly suggest picking up free-range, organic eggs from your local farmers' market and trying them fresh — these are very different in quality from what you can purchase in supermarkets. Very fresh eggs have a tighter egg white and their yolks are often a brighter orange/yellow than standard supermarket eggs — so much brighter, that if you're baking a vanilla cake, you may even notice the colour of the cake is slightly yellow.

Because I've done so much testing with eggs, I've found the amounts that work the best for the cakes I make. In some cases, my recipes call for half-egg amounts. This is a little unusual, but I do believe that exact amount produces the best result. To do this, simply beat an egg then halve it. Use one half for the cake and the other for a scrambled egg snack while you finish making the cake.

Solite

When I want to produce a really white frosted cake like the one on page 201, I use a product called Solite Creaming Shortening to achieve the look. There are two varieties of Solite available: one is a blend of animal and vegetable fats, the other a blend of vegetable fats only. I use the vegetable-only blend, which, when kept at room temperature, behaves similarly to butter. Like butter, it increases in volume when whipped. It's a really great option for vegans, or for people who require a lactose-free cake with icing. Most cake-decorating shops should have this, or an equivalent product. See page 204 for a Solite-based frosting.

Food colouring

Colour plays a huge role in the overall look of my cakes and desserts, and finding the type of colouring best-suited to the desserts you're making, and a brand you like using is very important. I've used liquid and powder colouring in the past, but I find AmeriColor's range of soft gel paste food colours produces the best variation in ombre colour palettes without splitting buttercreams or affecting the quality of meringues or macarons. Just a tiny amount of this gel produces a vibrant colour, so I find it's also good value for money, which is great when you are making a lot of desserts! I've used this brand throughout this book, but there are many good brands out there, and of course you can still use liquids and powders if you are after subtle pastel shades. Experiment to see what works for you.

Tips for working with AmeriColor Soft Gel Paste:

- When colouring buttercream or cake batter, always dip a skewer into the gel colour, and then dip that into the buttercream. This ensures you start with a very small amount. You can build the colour from there.

- When colouring Italian meringue (p. 108), I find it's good to add a drop of the gel to the boiling sugar water. This helps to reduce the gel and ensure it's not watery when added to the meringue later.

- If you want to blend a couple of colours together, do a trial run beforehand, and note down exactly how much of each colour you use.

Nuttelex

Nuttelex is an Australian brand of vegetarian and vegan spreads, and I use their 'Original' spread as a substitute for butter in most of my cake recipes. If you're unable to source Nuttelex, there are lots of similar products available at health or grocery stores. In my early twenties I started experimenting with this product due to some dietary intolerances. Since then, I've continued to use this product because it doesn't contain dairy, gluten, yeast, sucrose, nut oils, animal fats or artificial colours and flavours. It makes no difference to the quality of baked cakes and you can even use it as a substitute for butter in buttercreams and icing.

Flowers

Roses make great statement features on cakes, as do pretty little edible flowers. The different shades and shapes mean the design possibilities are endless.

If you want to use edible rose petals for decoration (p. 201), source them from a reliable supplier that can confirm the flowers are free from pesticides, chemicals and fertilisers. A good greengrocer or boutique fruit supplier will often stock packets of edible flowers that have been specifically grown for decorative purposes.

It's worth bearing in mind that the flavours will vary from flower to flower, and are subject to personal taste. Some varieties can be quite strong and too 'floral'. Ask the staff working in the shop for advice, or try one yourself to see if it suits your tastes.

TIP: You can freeze rose petals and other edible flowers until you're ready to use them for a special occasion. When using frozen flowers for an event or a dessert, it's best to apply them to the dessert just before serving, as they will begin to wilt and go soggy after a couple of hours. As an alternative, you can use crystallised flowers, or source non-edible flowers such as baby's breath, tropical flowers or green foliage, as they often have a longer life. Simply remove these decorative elements before eating.

First impressions

WE EAT WITH OUR EYES FIRST, so how you style your food and which props you use to set the scene are an integral part of making food and drinks look amazing. When we take pride in delivering something that has been carefully considered, it makes the experience even more special.

I have a lot of different types of props in my studio: cake stands, mugs, pretty spoons in lots of sizes, small and delicate dessert plates, fresh flowers, various colours of tissue paper, paints, balloons, small furniture items and so on. What I use varies depending on what I'm doing: photo shoots require very different looks from real-life events. In a picture, small props are the accessories to the desserts. They may not be the focus, but they provide a backdrop and help tell a story and bring dimension and balance to the image. In contrast, at events the dessert scene is viewed on a much larger scale. The focus is on creating an atmosphere and providing an experience using smaller props to create moments of surprise and delight once guests have absorbed the larger picture.

Styling is a very personal journey because it showcases your work and says a lot about who you are. There are no rules to how you style, so you have a lot of freedom when presenting your work; inspiration and ideas are endless, if you look for them. Texture, fine details and delicate and feminine lines are things that speak to me, so I look to replicate them, but in dessert form.

If you haven't identified your own style yet, here are a few tips to help you get started:

* Look around your home. What are your favourite items? Which colours do you gravitate towards?

* Once you have an idea of your style, keep an eye out for items that complement things you already have. Pretty tablecloths, a special cake slicer or a delicate cake stand. Build your collection over time and bring different pieces out for different times to mix and match.

* You don't need a photo shoot or fancy event to develop your style. Take every opportunity to spend just a little more time considering the details. Whether it's breakfast in bed, flowers on the dinner table or nice plates and napkins in a picnic basket, start small and build from there.

* Remember that small details can make a big impact. Colour-coordinate before you even start cooking.

I love finding ceramic and porcelain plates that are unique yet complement each other in tone and colour. A little bunch of flowers placed on the side of a place setting is also a sweet touch. Try to use flowers that don't wilt, especially if the weather is hot. Baby's breath works well, as do plants with tough leathery leaves, like eucalypts or acacias. Personalise things even further by styling each table setting with something for that guest. A small edible meringue wreath (p. 60) on a little dessert-plate setting makes a memorable impact.

Colour plays such an important role in styling. It should reflect or enhance the theme and mood of the event you are having.

Learning which colours work well together will help you create visual impact and make a great first impression when people arrive at your event, be it through props, flowers or the colour of the food and drinks being served.

A really good exercise when planning an event — and something I do often — is to get some pastels, paints or coloured pencils and sketch what you want your event/ table setting/dessert table or drinks trolley to look like. This can help crystallise in your mind which colours and props you want to use. Another great tip is to visit your local paint store and pick out some colour swatches you love. Take them home, mix and match to see what works well together and then go from there.

When working towards an event, it's also important to consider the layout of your table, especially when it comes to flowers. If you're adding little posies on plates, it's definitely worth speaking with a local florist a few weeks before the event about your colour and theme. Some flowers will be fine without refrigeration, while others need to be kept in some water in a fridge right up until the time of the event. Working all of this out will definitely save you time on the day and produce a beautiful result. Plan B is using beautiful green foliage or place cards.

Before an event, get your creative juices flowing by visiting:

- local charity shops to look for coloured glassware and interesting serving plates;

- ceramic stores to find small vessels or plates;

- hardware stores to look at metals and get ideas for interesting name-card holders;

- local nurseries to browse small succulents, flowers or greenery.

All of these places will have accessories you can use to add small details to an overall setting and create that personal touch for the guests at the table.

Setting the scene

THERE IS SOMETHING SO WHIMSICAL AND FEMININE ABOUT STEPPING OUTSIDE TO FIND A LITTLE TABLE DRESSED WITH FRESH FLOWERS AND DESSERT.

- Gold-coloured straws and spoons make a pretty statement next to so many colours.

- Rose petals on the side of your dessert plates are an easy way to decorate.

- Placing rugs on the grass and a linen cloth on the table, but not perfectly — a little off centre and scrunched — creates a more casual look.

- Little edible flowers in drinks will pretty them up.

- If the grass is dry, skip the table setting altogether and opt for some rugs and cushions under a large tree with some small vases and pretty flowers arranged in the centre.

- Always take your colour palette into consideration first; you don't need to use a lot of colours — just two or three in a few different shades.

Shooting your successes

SHOOT YOUR SUBJECT from different angles to get a feel for the lighting, how you want to tell the story and what your focal point is.

A CAMERA PHONE STICK is such a great tool to have, especially when shooting images to share on social media. It allows you to include your hands in the shot so you can style while you're taking the picture. This can give shots a more intimate and 'real-life' feel. A phone stick will also allow you to make stop-motion videos. An added bonus is that the phone is really stable, so your photos will come out perfectly.

ZOOMING IN allows you to capture images nice and close and gives a different perspective. I love doing this with flowers and intricate cake designs, as it shows so much detail.

LIFTING YOUR PHONE FURTHER AWAY is useful when you want to do 'flat lay' shots (overhead shots of objects arranged together). Don't forget to move around and take shots from different angles — the light will change, as will the perspective of the shot.

You may not always get the shot you want on the first try. Move things around, take photos from different angles, group things together and move them apart – you may end up with something that really surprises you.

When taking shots of food or drinks, I find it's best to shoot odd numbers — I typically shoot desserts, plates or drinks by themselves, or in groups of three.

Evening drives and travelling provide a totally different perspective from photography. Looking at how colours change, buildings light up and moods shift can be a great jumping-off point if you are searching for a way to challenge yourself when creating designs.

TAKING PHOTOGRAPHS OUTSIDE with your phone is a little different, mostly because the light is unfiltered, unlike shots taken indoors where windows, curtains or blinds help filter and control the light.

If the weather is slightly grey and dull, use the brightness function on your smartphone camera as well as the saturation and warmth functions (slide the controls up and down until you reach a level of colour you're happy with). I like to take photos in the Instagram app rather than use the camera function on my phone because I find it much quicker and easier to edit if the brightness needs to be adjusted. This also ensures you fit everything you want in Instagram's square format so you don't shoot a regular rectangular image that then needs to be cropped when you're ready to post it.

Also be clear on exactly what it is you're trying to capture. Is there anything in the picture you can remove or adjust to make the focal point stronger?

Layer one

MERINGUE JOURNEY

*Take pride in mastering the small details
in order to build a bigger picture*

in Layer one ...

MIRACLES IN MERINGUE

When I started working with eggs, the first layer in my journey was meringue – that beautiful light shell and crisp exterior that surprises you at first bite with its gooey, lush centre. It's a deceptive dessert on so many levels: it may seem simple and easy to make, but lots of things must work perfectly for it to turn out just right. This was frustrating at first, but the more I practised my techniques and tested recipes, the more I began to see patterns emerging in what worked and what didn't. I documented these things and began applying what I was learning to more interesting designs. I was able to continue to develop and evolve because I had a solid foundation from which to start.

BASIC MERINGUES

MAKES: 60 eeni mini meringues or 8 dessert-sized portions

PREP TIME: 5 minutes BAKING TIME: 20 minutes with a further
40 minutes drying in the oven

INGREDIENTS
- 2 egg whites
- 110 g (3¾ oz/½ cup) caster (superfine) sugar
- 1 teaspoon white vinegar
- flavoured extract or essence such as vanilla or strawberry (optional)
- a drop of AmeriColor Soft Gel Paste food colouring (optional)

EQUIPMENT
- 2 baking trays
- baking paper
- stand mixer with whisk attachment
- electric kitchen scales
- piping (icing) bag with pipe tip (see page 167 for suggestions)
- 2 wire racks

METHOD

1. Preheat the oven to 100°C (200°F) fan-forced (FF).

2. Line two trays with baking paper.

3. Using a stand mixer on high speed, whisk the egg whites until soft peaks form.

4. Reduce the speed to a medium setting and, using a tablespoon, add the sugar one tablespoon at a time until all of the sugar is added and the mixture is smooth and glossy.

5. Add the vinegar, the flavouring and the food colouring, if using. Whisk as before, on high speed for 3–5 minutes, or until the meringue has doubled in volume and the mixture is shiny.

6. Using a piping bag and piping tip of your choice, pipe a couple of dots directly onto the baking tray and place the baking paper on top. This will ensure that the baking paper doesn't move around.

7. If making eeni mini meringues, pipe 60 small rounds of meringue evenly onto your baking trays. Place the trays in the oven for 20 minutes.

8. After 20 minutes, turn the oven off and leave the meringues in the oven for a further 40 minutes.

9. When the time is up, remove the meringues from the oven, leave on the tray to cool for 10 minutes then carefully transfer to wire racks to cool completely.

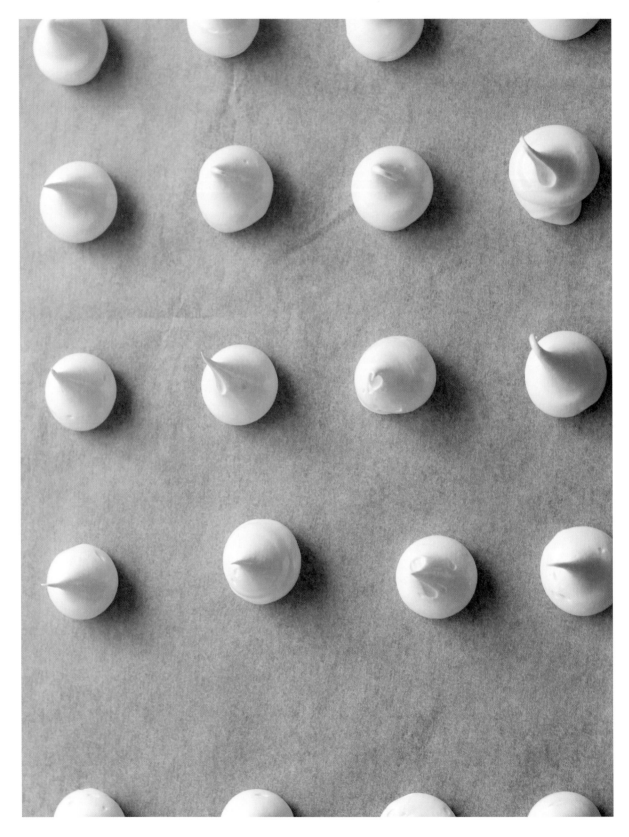

Balloons are such a fun way to celebrate an event.
I love buying them for no reason and using them
to decorate my office and studio. They have been a
great source of inspiration for my design work as well.
When turned upside down, they remind me of
light pillows — like meringues.

Two-tone meringues

Spoon half of the white meringue mixture from page 49 into a disposable piping (icing) bag fitted with pipe tip 1A. Pipe a tiny bit of meringue mixture onto your baking tray and then stick the baking paper on top to keep it from moving around. Pipe 30 white eeni mini meringues onto the tray.

Add a small drop of AmeriColor Soft Gel Paste in Dusty Rose to the remaining meringue mixture and beat using your stand mixer for a few seconds until the colour is evenly incorporated. Line another baking tray and pipe out 30 pink eeni mini meringues before cooking both trays of meringues in the oven, following the instructions on page 49.

Flowers are always a jumping-off point
for my designs — I'm constantly
taking photos of them for that reason.
I buy some every week, then arrange
them in vases around the house.
It's relaxing and allows creative energy
to flow through my work.

Surprise someone you love with
a box of rosette meringues

Lost in a **rose haze**

ALL THE BEAUTY I SEE

Lost in a **rose daze**

NOWHERE I WOULD RATHER BE

ROSETTE LOVE (P. 54)

METHOD

1. Preheat the oven to 100°C (200°F) (FF). Line two large baking trays with baking paper (dot some meringue directly on the tray to hold the paper in place). Add a drop of AmeriColor Soft Gel Paste in Red to the basic meringue mixture (p. 49) to get a very pale shade of pink.

2. Fill a piping (icing) bag fitted with pipe tip 22 with the pink meringue and pipe in an anticlockwise direction to create pretty rosettes. Repeat until you have 40–50 rosettes.

3. Bake for 20–22 minutes and then turn the oven off and leave the meringues in the cooling oven to dry out for 40 minutes, or until they are nice and crisp.

MERINGUE SHARDS

METHOD

1. Preheat the oven to 100°C (200°F) (FF). Line two large baking trays with baking paper (dot some meringue directly on the tray to hold the paper in place). Add a drop of AmeriColor Soft Gel Paste in Red to the basic meringue mixture (p. 49) to get a very pale shade of pink. Divide the mixture evenly between the two trays. Using a metal spatula, smear the meringue evenly over the trays to form a very thin paper-like layer.

2. Bake for 10 minutes and then turn the oven off and leave the meringues in the cooling oven to dry out for 20 minutes, or until they are nice and crisp. If it still seems still sticky after this time, turn the oven back on to 100°C (200°F) (FF) and bake for another 10–12 minutes before repeating the drying process.

3. Once the meringue has dried out, remove from the oven, allow to cool and then break into shards. You can use these shards to decorate cakes, ice creams, cupcakes and waffles.

PRETTY PAVLOVAS

1 Preheat the oven to 100°C (200°F) (FF). Using an 8 cm (3¼ inch) cookie cutter, trace six circles, evenly spaced, on good-quality baking paper. Make them dark enough so the outline shows on the other side. Flip the baking paper over.

2 Spoon a heaped tablespoon of the basic meringue mixture (p. 49) onto each circle.

3 With a small metal spatula, spread and smooth out each meringue and create a small dip in the centre of each one. Bake for 40 minutes, then turn the oven off and leave the meringues in there to dry for 1 hour.

4 I like to make mini pavlovas by topping my meringues with whipped cream, double cream or crème fraîche before adding some drizzles of Pretty-in-pink Rhubarb Syrup (p. 232) and fresh fruit.

Pavlovas with whipped cream, rhubarb syrup and fresh strawberries.

pavlovas

should have a soft, luscious and gooey centre
and be crisp on the outside

Styling with meringue wreaths

These playful and pretty wreaths are so easy to make and versatile to use when styling. Serve them on small plates at Christmas with a name card in the middle for each guest, or hang them from your Christmas tree for fun, edible decorations.

For a gorgeous dessert, whip some cream and add a dollop to the centre of each wreath then garnish with some fresh berries.

They also look great on top of the eeni mini cakes (p. 170). You can use different pipe tips, as I've done here, or one pipe tip. These can be made up to three days ahead of time and stored in an airtight container if you want to get ahead.

MAKING MERINGUE WREATHS

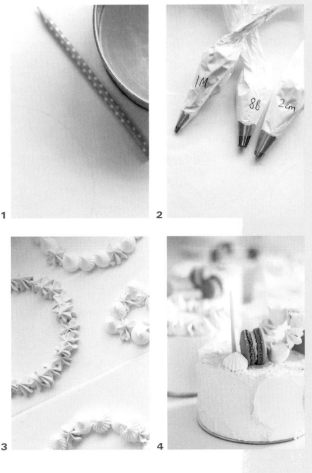

1. Use a 15 cm (6 inch) round cake tin to trace a circle on baking paper — make it dark enough that it shows through the other side. To make smaller wreaths, you can use an 8 cm (3¼ inch) round cookie cutter or even a mug to trace the circle. Depending on how many wreaths you want, you may need to double the meringue recipe. The basic recipe (p. 49) will yield about three 15 cm wreaths or six to eight smaller ones.

2. You'll need a skewer, three piping (icing) bags, three different pipe tips: 1M, 8B and a 2 cm (¾ inch) round tip, and AmeriColor Soft Gel Paste in Dusty Rose. Use a skewer to add a tiny dot of colour to the meringue, mix it in well, then put one-third of the meringue into your piping bag. Repeat this step to achieve slightly darker colours.

3. Flip the baking paper over and, using the different piping bags, pipe along the outlines of the circles, alternating between bags so you get a mix of colours and shapes. Ensure the meringues are touching each other as you go. Bake according to the instructions on page 49.

4. Use for decorating cakes, table settings, even hot chocolates.

Layer two

CUPCAKE JOURNEY

Repeating delicate details crafts unforgettable impact

in Layer two ...

MY FIRST LOVE

My journey with cupcakes is very special to me. I remember when I first started baking and eating them as a child. Like those of many other kids, my cupcakes were decorated with chocolate icing, musk sticks and colourful sprinkles. I used to beg my mother to let me lick the spatula and mixing bowl when we'd finished with them, an experience I imagine many have shared.

When I started baking cupcakes for my own business some years ago, I didn't realise how distinctive my decorating style was: I had a very soft, dainty, feminine aesthetic. For me, it was all about the finer details. I started creating collections of what I call my 'eeni mini cupcakes' and I worked hard to perfect the style of the icing, using specific shades and colours that would eventually become my signature 'look'. I experimented by adding delicate details like sprinkles mixed together with sugar sands, which added special details not seen before. Small touches of gold leaf gave them that luxurious look.

I wanted to photograph these little desserts in the same level of detail that had gone in to making them, and I wanted to celebrate this creative journey with a community who would appreciate the effort and time I was putting in to the process. My style of dessert design and photography has become quite well known since then — many people who have seen my work in person or on Instagram now recognise my images without seeing my name. I feel very privileged and humbled to know that people have an affection for what I do, and even celebrate it.

BASIC CUPCAKES

MAKES: 6 large cupcakes or 24 eeni mini cupcakes

PREP TIME: 10 minutes BAKING TIME: 22 minutes (for large), 14 minutes (for eeni mini)

INGREDIENTS

- 100 g (3½ oz) caster (superfine) sugar
- 120 g (4½ oz) plain (all-purpose) flour
- ½ teaspoon baking powder
- 40 g (1¼ oz) Nuttelex or unsalted butter, softened
- 120 ml (4 fl oz/½ cup) milk
- 1 egg
- 1 teaspoon vanilla extract or essence

EQUIPMENT

- 6-hole large cupcake or muffin tray (for large cupcakes) or 24-hole mini muffin tray (for eeni mini cupcakes)
- 6 large or 24 mini paper cupcake cases
- electric kitchen scales
- sieve
- stand mixer with whisk attachment
- measuring jug and spoons
- whisk
- silicone spatula
- wire rack

METHOD

1. Preheat the oven to 160°C (315°F) fan-forced (FF).

2. Line a cupcake tray with paper cupcake cases.

3. Sift all the dry ingredients into the bowl of a stand mixer, then add the Nuttelex (or butter).

4. Gently whisk the milk, egg and vanilla together in a measuring jug.

5. Turn the stand mixer on to a low speed and mix until the ingredients have formed a dry crumb, then gradually add the milk mixture.

6. Once all of the milk mixture has been incorporated, turn up to high speed for 1 minute, or until the mixture is smooth. If required, turn off, scrape down the sides of the bowl, then mix for a few seconds more.

7. Using a metal tablespoon (or teaspoon for eeni minis), evenly distribute the batter between the paper cupcake cases, leaving about 5 mm (¼ inch) at the top.

8. Place in the middle of the oven and bake for 22 minutes (14 minutes, if baking eeni mini cupcakes).

9. Once baked, leave the cupcakes in the tray for 5–6 minutes before removing to a wire rack to cool completely.

EASY FLAVOUR VARIATIONS

- Add the finely grated zest of 1 lemon or orange to the basic batter.
- Mix 25 g (1 oz) of unsweetened cocoa powder into the batter. Push a small square of dark chocolate into each cupcake before baking.
- Push a fresh berry into the centre of each cupcake and ensure it is covered with batter before baking.

BASIC BUTTERCREAM

MAKES: 600 g (1 lb 5 oz), enough to decorate 6 large cupcakes,
24 eeni mini cupcakes or enough to fill and decorate
one eeni mini cake (p. 152)
You'll need a double batch of this buttercream to fill and ice
one celebration cake (p. 184)
PREP TIME: 5 minutes

INGREDIENTS
- 125 g (4½ oz/½ cup) softened unsalted butter (see note)
- 500 g (1 lb 2 oz) soft icing mixture, sifted
- 50 ml (1½ fl oz) milk
- 1 teaspoon vanilla extract or essence
- food colouring (optional)

EQUIPMENT
- electric kitchen scales
- measuring jug
- sieve
- measuring spoons
- stand mixer with whisk attachment
- silicone spatula

METHOD
Add all of the ingredients to the bowl of a stand mixer and beat until light and fluffy, about 4–5 minutes.

NOTE If you are dairy intolerant, replace the butter with Nuttelex (see page 31) or an equivalent product and use soy milk as an alternative to milk.

TIP   If not using immediately, say for 1 or 2 hours, cover with plastic wrap directly on the buttercream and leave at room temperature. Before using, whisk again and add a drop of milk to loosen, if needed. If making ahead, this can also be refrigerated for up to 3 days. Again, just make sure the plastic wrap is touching the buttercream, allow to come to room temperature and whisk again before using, adding a drop of milk if needed.

When creaming butter and sugar, you want to make sure it is pale, light in texture and fluffy.

simply iced

the beginnings of a
perfectly iced cupcake

Styling with buttercream

Beautifully applied buttercream is the crown on a perfectly baked cupcake. If your cupcakes have been slightly chilled in the fridge, you'll find the buttercream goes on a lot easier because it starts to set as you're smoothing it out, which helps make the application much neater.

Holding a small metal spatula at an angle, apply the buttercream so it forms a smooth cone before levelling it off at the top. Keep a small bowl of buttercream by your side, as you may require more or need to wipe off excess as you go.

CONCEPT BUILDING
Cupcake Collection

My travels to America provided me with so many rich visual experiences. Camera in hand, I captured photos of colour combinations I was drawn to. The turquoise and pink of this ice-cream truck, the neon pink taco sign and white buildings against beautiful blue skies became the inspiration for this collection of little cupcakes.

MAKE A BATCH OF EENI MINI CUPCAKES (p. 67) and a batch of the basic buttercream (p. 68). Prepare three piping (icing) bags with three different pipe tips: 1M, 1A and 4B. Tip 1M will give you a star or rosette, 1A a smooth round look and 4B will produce an open star look (see opposite). You'll also need AmeriColor Soft Gel Pastes in Dusty Rose and Turquoise; cocoa powder; 20 g (¾ oz) of good-quality dark chocolate and a little clear sugar sand.

DECIDE WHICH PIPE TIP TO USE for each colour of buttercream before you start decorating. Halve the buttercream and mix 1 tablespoon of cocoa powder into one half then spoon that into a piping bag. Divide the plain buttercream in half, mixing a drop of Dusty Rose into one half, and a small drop of Turquoise into the other. Spoon into your piping bags then pipe onto the cupcakes in pretty combinations. Finish with shaved chocolate or a sprinkle of sugar sand.

CUPCAKE COLLECTION

CUPCAKE WITH THE
LOT TO GO-GO

These are **eeni mini cupcakes** (p. 67) decorated using **buttercream** (p. 68) tinted with **AmeriColor Soft Gel Paste in Turquoise**; you'll need to add a few drops of the colour to get this dark hue. Start with one drop and keep adding until you get the desired colour. Use round pipe tip 12 to apply the buttercream in an anticlockwise direction, moving your hand in an upward motion when you are on top of the previous layer of icing. To finish, add **half a macaron shell** (p. 108), a **rosette love meringue** (p. 56) and **a mini dark chocolate cookie**.

WHEN CUPCAKE MEETS MERINGUE:
SIMPLY KISSED

For this variation, I iced **larger cupcakes** (p. 67) with **buttercream** (p. 68) tinted with just a hint of **AmeriColor Soft Gel Paste in Turquoise** to create a very pale shade of greeny-blue. After using the simply iced technique (p. 71), I added some **little meringue kisses**, made by joining two **mini meringues** (p. 49) together with a little buttercream. When applying the kisses to the cupcakes, I like to tilt them slightly to the side so they are on varying angles. Sprinkle over some **clear sugar sand** to finish.

CONTRASTING SHADES

Using pale shades of black and turquoise
to create three different looks.

COLOURS

I added a drop of AmeriColor Soft Gel Paste in Black to half a batch of buttercream (p. 68) to make the grey colour, and just a hint of AmeriColor Soft Gel Paste in Turquoise to the other half to create this very pale shade of blue.

OPTION 1

Use the simply iced decorating technique (p. 71) with the pale turquoise buttercream. Then use pipe tip 1M with the grey icing. Hold the piping (icing) bag vertical to the cupcake, and push a little star shape on top.

OPTION 2

The main colour here is the grey. Using pipe tip 1M, pipe a rose onto each cupcake then use a metal spatula to smooth out the bottom and sides, like the simply iced cupcake (p. 71), leaving a tiny bit of the rose work on top. Add a little turquoise buttercream (just a hint) as a smear on one side of the cupcake to create the contrast.

OPTION 3

Start by using the pale turquoise buttercream to make a simply iced cupcake (p. 71), then smear a tiny bit of grey buttercream around the cupcake when you smooth and finish off.

Observing how different colours interact in nature, and taking photographs of flowers in gardens, nurseries and parks is a great way to build your knowledge of colour play.

COTTON CANDY CUPCAKES

These pretty **cupcakes** (p. 67) have been decorated with **edible violas**, which look beautiful as a garnish on a simply iced cupcake (p. 71) with a **halved strawberry** and a sprinkle of **clear sugar sand**. Add 1–2 drops of **fairy floss (cotton candy) essence** to the **basic buttercream** (p. 68) along with a tiny drop of **AmeriColor Soft Gel Paste in Deep Pink** for colour. The essence is concentrated, so start with a drop and always taste before adding more.

Layer three

DONUT JOURNEY

She was making the ordinary extraordinary

in layer three ...

THE PLAYFUL DONUT

There are always squeals of delight when guests walk into a room to find trays of colourful iced donuts waiting for them. There's something unexpected and fun about this particular dessert. And the best part is they also happen to be very easy to make. When decorated, they can be very pretty additions to an event or special occasion. Deep-fried donuts are the norm, and they are delicious, but I prefer making baked donuts using slightly healthier ingredients, which make no compromise on flavour.

If you haven't made donuts before, try baking a batch for your next event instead of your usual biscuits or cupcakes. Once they are out of the oven, rope a few friends, your partner or your children into decorating them with you. Form an assembly line and you'll have trays of beautiful donuts ready in no time.

BASIC DONUTS

MAKES: 12–14 donuts

PREP TIME: 10 minutes BAKING TIME: 10–12 minutes.

INGREDIENTS
- 150 g (5½ oz) Nuttelex or unsalted butter, softened
- 110 g (3¾ oz/½ cup) caster (superfine) sugar
- 1 egg
- 60 ml (2 fl oz/¼ cup) milk
- 60 g (2¼ oz) plain yoghurt, or yoghurt with a sweet flavoured syrup like strawberry, rhubarb or watermelon
- 1 teaspoon vanilla extract or essence
- 190 g (6¾ oz) plain (all-purpose) flour
- 2 teaspoons baking powder
- ½ teaspoon bicarbonate of soda (baking soda)
- 1 teaspoon ground cinnamon
- canola oil cooking spray

EQUIPMENT
- electric kitchen scales
- stand mixer with whisk attachment
- measuring jug and spoons
- large piping (icing) bag with large piping tip 1A
- 2 or 3 donut baking tins (how many you need will depend on how many holes the tins have)
- 2 wire racks

METHOD
1. Preheat the oven to 170°C (325°F) fan-forced (FF).

2. Place the Nuttelex (or butter) and sugar in the bowl of a stand mixer and whisk on a low then medium speed until light and fluffy.

3. With the mixer still going, add the egg, milk, yoghurt and vanilla, and mix until just combined.

4. Add the flour, baking powder, bicarbonate of soda and cinnamon, and mix until a soft dough has formed — this should only take 1 minute. Scrape down the bowl, if necessary, to ensure all the ingredients have combined evenly.

5. Place the dough in a piping bag fitted with a piping tip.

6. Evenly spray the donut tins with canola spray.

7. Using firm pressure, pipe the dough into the donut holes ensuring it only comes three-quarters of the way up each hole.

8. Bake for 10–12 minutes, or until lightly golden.

9. Remove from the oven and allow to cool in the tin for a few minutes before turning out onto a wire rack. Allow to cool down fully before you start decorating.

There's nothing quite like a tray of freshly baked donuts.
Allow them to cool down completely on a wire rack
before you start decorating them.

OMBRE ICED DONUTS

CONCEPT BUILDING
Ombre Iced Donuts

I love looking at shapes and patterns in the world around me and linking them in my mind with a particular dessert. When I find myself wandering through streets where there are beautiful buildings, I take photos from different angles, observing the design and style of even the smallest details.

THIS BEAUTIFUL BUILDING is a pale shade of pink embellished with gorgeous arched windows, a striking feature that perfectly accentuates the shape of the building.

IT BECAME THE STARTING POINT for a very simple but pretty donut design — one that perfectly illustrates how simple shapes can make a grander statement, especially when grouped or lined up together and decorated in the same colour, or in slight variations of a colour.

OMBRE ICED DONUTS

This icing will easily make enough for 12 donuts.
You want to make sure that you have a good amount of icing
to dip your donuts in. To achieve this ombre look, you need to create
grades of one colour in the same family, starting from the lightest
tone and working to the darkest. Start with just a little colouring
at the beginning because you can only go darker from there.

OMBRE ICING

INGREDIENTS
- 400 g (14 oz) pure icing (confectioners') sugar
- 125 ml (4 fl oz/½ cup) water
- flavouring: extract or essence of your choice (optional)
- AmeriColor Soft Gel Paste in Dusty Rose (or any other colour you like)

EQUIPMENT
- electric kitchen scales
- sieve
- stand mixer with whisk attachment
- metal tablespoon
- metal spatula

METHOD

1. Sift the sugar into the bowl of your stand mixer.

2. Mix on a low speed, slowly adding one tablespoon of water at a time. If you add too much water at the start, you may end up with a really runny icing. The consistency you are looking for when making this icing is thick like honey, so the slower you add the water, the easier this is to monitor. You may find that you don't need to use the all the water. If you find that the water is not enough, add some more — again in a controlled way, adding a little at a time.

3. Once you feel the mixture has the right consistency, turn the mixer up to high speed for 2 minutes, add a little capful of flavouring (if using) and a drop of colour to make the icing the lightest shade of the colours you are going to create.

4. If your donuts are still warm, pop them in the freezer on a wire rack for 12 minutes so they get really cold before you start dipping them in the icing. This helps the glaze set quickly and gives a more polished look. To achieve an ombre look on the donuts, dip a donut into the bowl of icing so it is halfway in, not completely submerged. Apply a tiny bit of pressure then be gentle when removing. You may want to use a small metal spatula to help lift it until you get the hang of it. Repeat with a few more.

5. Once you have iced a few donuts in the first shade of colour, simply add a drop more of the same colouring to the icing, whisk in well, then ice a few more donuts. Tint the icing darker still, then ice a few more. Continue until the icing is used up.

6. If you find that your icing is getting a little dry, add a small amount of water to the icing and whisk for a few seconds.

DONUT #FLATLAY

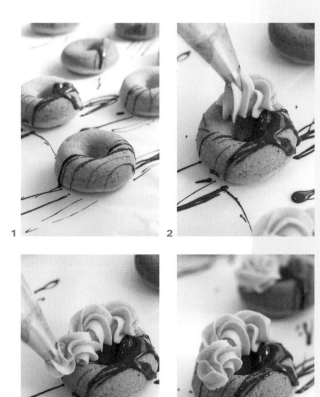

To achieve this look, you'll need a piping (icing) bag fitted with pipe tip 1M.

Melt 100 g (3½ oz) of good-quality dark chocolate in a microwave in 10-second blasts until completely smooth and melted. Alternatively, place the chocolate in a heatproof bowl and sit it over a small saucepan of simmering water; don't let the water touch the base of the bowl. Melt the chocolate until smooth, stirring gently.

1 Dip a fork into the hot melted chocolate and wave it back and forth over each donut to create a beautiful free-flowing drizzle of melted chocolate. Allow to cool completely before proceeding with the decorating.

2 Make a basic buttercream (p. 68) then add 1 small drop of Wilton Color Paste in Red (or feel free to use whatever suits your needs). You can add more colour if you are after a deeper shade of pink.

3 Hold the piping (icing) bag on a 65-degree angle as you pipe swirls on the sides of the donuts. Rotate the piping bag in an anticlockwise direction three times per donut.

Reaching up for the sky,
trees provide beautiful lines and patterns

rosewater donut ice creams

DONUT WORRIES (P. 94)

These very cute donuts are fun additions to any party. They always put a smile on people's faces, and they disappear very quickly.

METHOD

1. Add ½ a capful of strawberry essence to the Ombre Icing (p. 90). Tint the icing with a tiny bit of AmeriColor Soft Gel Paste in Dusty Rose to create a pale pink.

2. To decorate, add some edible eyes, a mini meringue (p. 49), touches of gold leaf, some white sprinkles and a dusting of crushed meringue.

ROSEWATER DONUT ICE CREAMS (P. 95)

Some time ago, I fused my love for donuts and ice cream together to create these little desserts. They are so pretty and have been super-popular on Instagram, and through my business.

METHOD

1. Add ½ a capful of rosewater essence to the Ombre Icing (p. 90). Tint the icing with a tiny bit of AmeriColor Soft Gel Paste in Dusty Rose to create a pale pink.

2. To decorate, start by sticking ice-cream cones to the donuts (see note about ice-cream cones on page 126): dip the widest part of the cone into the icing mixture and then stick that onto the side of the donut to 'glue' it together. Leave for 10 minutes to set. You may need to use the back of a spoon to prop up the cone until so it stays level while it sets.

3. Gently 'glue' two mini meringues onto the icing and add some touches of gold leaf and a sprinkle of crushed meringue. These are best served on individual small plates.

Styling with tins

My basic donut recipe (p. 86) is versatile in that you can use similar-sized tins and moulds with different patterns to change the visual story. There is a variety of bundt tins out there that will create beautiful lines on a donut. As each tin is different, and because you may pipe your mixture thinner or thicker, baking times will vary. Start by baking the donuts at 170°C (325°F) (FF) for 9 minutes, then check on them every minute after that until you work out the correct baking time for that particular tin. Don't let all your hard work go to waste! Keep track of your experiments in a little notebook or on your smartphone so you don't have to start from the beginning the next time.

The lines on donuts baked in a bundt tin are sharp, and a lovely contrast to the round shape. For extra beauty, drizzle teaspoonfuls of light pink icing (p. 90) over the donuts, swaying your hand back and forth. Garnish with a mini meringue (p. 49) and a few shavings of dark chocolate.

CONCEPT BUILDING

Tiffany-Rose Was Her Name

I was actually at a meeting in a small, quaint street with my publisher, discussing this book, when I spotted this tree of dainty pink flowers. I absolutely love it when the skies are bright blue, and I started to imagine how the flowers might look with that colour behind them. That image in my mind became the artistic anchor for these special and sophisticated donuts.

MAKE THE OMBRE ICING (p. 90), then add some vanilla extract or essence and enough AmeriColor Soft Gel Paste in Turquoise to achieve the vibrant solid turquoise colour seen opposite.

DIP THE DONUTS IN THE ICING as on page 90, then add a little edible rosette to each donut. If you aren't sure how to make these, there are great videos online that will walk you through it step by step. Alternatively, specialty cake stores should sell them. Sprinkle over some crushed meringue (p. 56) to finish.

TIFFANY-ROSE WAS HER NAME

Trust in your patience and persistence — and the knowledge gained from your mistakes.

in Layer four ...

THE MIGHTY MACARON

One of the more difficult desserts to make, and one that
almost defeated me. I had some epic failures in the early stages
of learning how to make macarons.

The journey was a frustrating one, but these delicate and pretty
little desserts are really a testament to you if you can persevere
and master them. It took me some time to get them right and
I had to learn from my mistakes, many of which I'll share in this layer.
Tools are really important for this dessert — not only having the
right ones, but also making sure you know your equipment really well
and being thoughtful in your approach to it. This is something
I wish I'd known from the start, as trying to perfect these
almost put me off baking altogether.

Thanks to my husband's can-do attitude and encouragement,
I picked myself up and refocused. I learned from the mistakes and
made changes and improvements. I started to document
all that was happening and eventually I mastered this tough
little dessert. I'm so glad I did, and you will be, too.
There's truly nothing quite like eating a fresh macaron.

It seemed impossible, until it was done

THE FIRST TIME I MADE MACARONS IT WAS A DISASTER. Without going into too much detail, they cracked. I tried to make them five more times with no success, and I couldn't quite work out what I was doing wrong. After a few tears, and on the verge of quitting, I decided to take a break and troubleshoot what was happening in my kitchen.

MY FIRST INSTINCT WAS THAT MY EQUIPMENT WAS FAILING ME. Until this point, I'd been making do with what I had in the kitchen but, after reading a few online baking forums, I started to think that perhaps some essential pieces of equipment were missing. The first was the sieve. I had a few already, but they each struggled to sift the almond meal. Then I remembered seeing a drum sieve being used to make purées on TV, and that got me thinking that perhaps the mesh would be larger than in the sieves I had. I was also eyeballing the mixture when making the sugar syrup for the meringue — in other words, 'guesstimating' when it had reached 100°C (200°F) based on how the syrup looked. But I wasn't sure what I was looking for, so how could I really know?

AT THIS POINT, I DECIDED TO GO TO A PROPER CHEFS' SUPPLY STORE AND BUY A SUGAR THERMOMETER AND A DRUM SIEVE. This would at least ensure that my temperature was accurate and that my ingredients would be sifted properly. Perhaps this seems like a fairly obvious decision to make from the start, but I honestly believe that many people think they can wing it with what they have in the kitchen. That's why I want to break everything down to basics here, so the importance of having the right equipment for the right job is clear and understood.

I ALSO THOUGHT THAT MY BAKING TRAYS WERE PLAYING A ROLE IN AFFECTING THE 'FEET' OF THE MACARONS. 'Foot' refers to the little ruffles around the edge of a macaron. When made correctly, these are uniform in size and look really pretty. I'm not sure what prompted to me to think this other than remembering that my trays felt really hot. Perhaps my oven temperature and trays were wreaking havoc on the macarons. I started to trial different trays until I found one that worked really well.

AFTER TACKLING THE EQUIPMENT, I TURNED MY ATTENTION TO THE SECOND ISSUE: INGREDIENTS. What sung out to me was egg whites. I'd previously observed that the egg whites I used were runny at times, and thick at others. I'd also read articles highlighting the importance egg whites play in macarons. Until this point, I'd thought that as long as the eggs I used were good-quality, fresh and organic, that was enough. But if my egg whites were good-quality, why were they failing me? I decided to perform my own trials based on the age of the eggs. So I purchased a couple of dozen eggs and every few days I made a batch of macarons, assessing whether there was any improvement in the result. I also decided to purchase egg albumen — this is the white of an egg, but in powdered form. It helps to stabilise the fresh egg whites when they are being beaten. These experiments proved that using an older egg significantly improves the macarons. For me, the best results come from using eggs that are five days before their best-before date.

ITALIAN MERINGUE

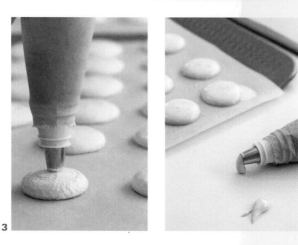

1 When whisking Italian meringue, you want to ensure that the sugar syrup is poured in a slow, steady stream while the mixer is running on a low–medium speed. I highly recommend using a timer and setting it to 10 minutes once you have finished adding your sugar syrup, then turning the speed to high to whisk until the timer goes off. When finished, the meringue should have a lovely glossy shine to it.

2 Macaronage — this is the lava-like consistency you want to achieve (see below).

3 Using even, steady pressure, pipe 3 cm (1¼ inch) rounds on the tray about the same distance apart.

A MINI MACARON GLOSSARY

ITALIAN VS FRENCH MERINGUE: For an Italian meringue, sugar and water are boiled together then whisked into egg whites until firm peaks form. This meringue is used for macarons, icing cakes and for mousses. For a French meringue, egg whites and sugar are beaten together until light and airy, often with cream of tartar or vinegar to help stabilise the mixture.

MACARONAGE: The lava-like consistency achieved by working the batter so that it's slightly loose, smooth and shiny. There is a fine line between perfect and overworked, because if you take it too far, it will become very runny. It needs to be thick and slowly running off the spatula. To test it, you can run your spatula down the middle of the batter and make a line. Count to five, and if the batter merges together in that time, it's ready.

CROUTAGE: Allowing the piped macarons to dry after they've been baked. They should develop a thin dry film on the shell once they've had sufficient time to dry out. Your finger should be able to touch the macaron shells without lifting off any of the mixture. I like to dry my macarons in the oven on a very low temperature.

BASIC MACARONS
(ITALIAN MERINGUE METHOD)

MAKES: 30 filled macarons

PREP TIME: 30 minutes BAKING TIME: 11–12 minutes

INGREDIENTS
- 200 g (7 oz) almond meal
- 190 g (6¾ oz) soft icing mixture or icing (confectioners') sugar
- 165 g (5¾ oz) egg whites (for macarons, I use eggs that are 5 days before their best-before date)
- ¼ teaspoon powdered egg albumen (see page 104)
- 200 g (7 oz) caster (superfine) sugar
- a drop of AmeriColor Soft Gel Paste if you want pastel-hued macarons (optional)

EQUIPMENT
- electric kitchen scales
- drum sieve
- large stainless-steel bowl
- stand mixer with whisk attachment
- heavy-based saucepan
- sugar thermometer
- silicone spatula
- piping (icing) bag with pipe tip 12
- 2–4 baking trays (depending on how you space your piped macarons as you pipe them)
- good-quality baking paper
- damp clean tea towel
- plastic scraper
- 2 wire racks

METHOD
1. Preheat the oven to 60°C (140°F) fan-forced (FF).

2. Measure the almond meal and soft icing mixture then, using a drum sieve, sift both ingredients twice into a large stainless-steel mixing bowl. Set aside. (Trust me, doing this twice is very important.)

3. Add half of the egg whites to the mixing bowl with the almond meal mixture then set aside. Place the other half in the bowl of a stand mixer.

4. Add the powdered egg albumen to the bowl of the stand mixer.

5. Put the caster sugar in heavy-based saucepan with 70 ml (2¼ fl oz) of cold water. Place the sugar thermometer in the saucepan and set it to 100°C (200°F), then turn the heat up to high.

6. When the sugar syrup reaches 100°C (200°F), add one drop of colour to it, and then set the sugar thermometer to 108°C (226°F).

7. When the sugar syrup reaches temperature, increase the sugar thermometer temperature to its final setting: 114°C (237°F). While that is coming up to temperature, turn the stand mixer to the highest setting and whisk the egg whites until soft peaks form.

8.   When the sugar syrup reaches temperature, remove the saucepan from the heat and allow the syrup to cool for a few seconds. Reduce the stand mixer speed to slow and slowly pour in the sugar syrup. Increase the speed to high and beat the mixture for 10 minutes.

9.   Using your spatula, incorporate the remaining egg white into the almond meal and icing sugar mixture until a thick paste has formed.

10. Once the stand mixer has been going for 10 minutes, turn it off. Remove the whisk attachment and tap (quite aggressively) the small amount of mixture that is on the whisk into the large bowl of almond paste. Mix this meringue into the almond paste to loosen it.

11. Add the remaining meringue to the paste and gently fold it through until fully mixed. This process should take 3–4 minutes. What you are trying to achieve is a thick lava-like mixture that has a good shine to it (see page 106 for more guidance). Excessive mixing will result in a really loose batter, which will cause your macarons to spread out after they are piped.

PIPING AND BAKING
THE MACARONS

METHOD

1.   Place half of this mixture into a piping bag, ensuring your pipe tip is inserted first.

2.   Place 4 small dots of meringue in each corner of each baking tray, then place a sheet of baking paper on top to 'glue' it down.

3.   Pipe 3 cm (1¼ inch) rounds on the tray about the same distance apart. Depending on the size of your oven and trays, you should be able to fit 30 shells on one tray, even with a small oven.

4.   Repeat the same process with the next tray.

5.   Place the trays in the oven and leave for 7 minutes to air-dry — if the humidity is quite high in the room, you may need to dry the macarons longer, possibly up to 20 minutes. When they have dried, you should be able to touch them and have no batter come off on your fingers. I suggest touching one at the front of the tray and one in the middle.

6.   Once the macarons are dry, remove the trays from the oven and place onto wire racks. (The kitchen bench top may be cold, and this can cause the macarons to deflate. Wire racks prevent this shock.) Turn the oven up to 160°C (315°F) (FF).

7.   Once the oven is up to temperature, return the macarons to the oven for 11–12 minutes.

8.   Remove from the oven and gently move the baking paper off each tray and onto a damp tea towel.

9.   Using a scraper, carefully transfer the macarons to wire racks to cool completely.

10. The shells will keep in an airtight container for 4 days in the fridge. You can also freeze them with no filling for 2 months. If you choose to do this, remove them from the freezer, place in the fridge for 12 hours to defrost, then add filling and consume within 24 hours.

The biggest lesson in my baking journey has been that timing is everything. Being patient, not rushing a process and understanding why I need to wait have been crucial to my development as a baker. If you want to make a dessert for a special occasion and suspect you might have to rush, choose something simple.

decadent white ganache

THREE GREAT FILLINGS

*These all take 10 minutes to make, and keep for
up to 5 days in the fridge.*

GANACHE

MAKES: 1 dessert-sized bowl (350 g/12 oz), enough to fill 30+ macarons

INGREDIENTS

- 180 ml (6 fl oz/¾ cup) thickened (whipping) cream
- 200 g (7 oz) good-quality dark chocolate (70% cocoa) or
  white couverture chocolate, roughly chopped
- 20 g (¾ oz) unsalted butter

METHOD

Bring 300 ml (10½ fl oz) of water to the boil in a heavy-based saucepan. Place the cream in a heatproof bowl that fits on top of the saucepan. Put the chocolate into another heatproof bowl and set aside. Place the bowl of cream over the water (make sure the water doesn't touch the bottom of the bowl), reduce the heat to medium and allow the cream to almost reach boiling point. Pour the cream over the chocolate and stir until the chocolate has completely melted into the hot cream. (If it doesn't melt, place the heatproof bowl back onto the saucepan, but don't turn the heat on.) Add the butter and stir until melted. Allow to cool slightly before placing plastic wrap directly onto the ganache, then chill in the refrigerator until firm. Let it come to room temperature then whisk before using.

GOOEY CARAMEL

MAKES: 1 dessert-sized bowl (200 g/7 oz) enough to fill 30+ macarons

INGREDIENTS

- 40 g (1½ oz) unsalted butter
- 80 g (2¾ oz) soft brown sugar
- 100 ml (3½ fl oz) thick (double) cream
- 1 tablespoon golden syrup or treacle

METHOD

Place all the ingredients in a heavy-based saucepan over a high heat. Bring to the boil, then reduce the heat and simmer for 2 minutes. Spoon into a bowl, allow to cool a little, then place plastic wrap directly onto the caramel and allow to set in the fridge for a few hours.

STRAWBERRY JAM

MAKES: 1 medium jar (450 g/1 lb) enough to fill 30+ macarons

INGREDIENTS

- 250 g (9 oz) strawberries, hulled and halved
- 300 g (10½ oz) caster (superfine) sugar
- juice of ½ a lemon (add more if the mixture seems dry)

METHOD

Place all the ingredients in heavy-based saucepan over a high heat and bring to the boil. After 2 minutes, turn the heat down and simmer for 5–6 minutes, stirring occasionally. Pour into a sterilised jar and allow to cool for 5 minutes. Place some plastic wrap on top of the jar then screw the lid on. Refrigerate until needed.

STRAWBERRY TOP HAT MACARONS

These cheerful little desserts are a really simple way of serving macarons and the effect can be quite striking. Because only one **macaron shell** (p. 108) is required for each serving, they're perfect for large events and celebrations — just a few batches of macaron shells can serve a lot of people, and they really show off the beautiful fruit. Pipe simple **vanilla buttercream** (p. 68) or **dark chocolate ganache** (p. 113) onto the shells using a piping (icing) bag fitted with pipe tip 12 and then top with **fresh strawberry halves**.

CARAMEL MACARONS WITH PINK SALT

FOR 15 FILLED MACARONS YOU WILL NEED:

- piping (icing) bag with pipe tip 12
- 300 g (10½ oz) basic buttercream (about ½ a batch) (p. 68)
- 30 macaron shells (p. 108)
- gooey caramel (p. 113)
- pink Himalayan sea salt

METHOD

1. Pipe the buttercream in an anticlockwise direction around the around the periphery of 15 macaron shells, leaving their centres empty.

2. Drop ½ a teaspoon of caramel into the centre of each macaron followed by a small sprinkle of the pink salt. Put the empty shells on top of their filled partners and press down gently to make 15 macarons. Place in the fridge to set and then serve, preferably that day, but these will keep in an airtight container for 4 days.

STRAWBERRY-CENTRE MACARONS (P. 114)

FOR 15 MACARONS YOU WILL NEED:

- piping (icing) bag with pipe tip 12
- 300 g (10½ oz) basic buttercream (about ½ a batch) (p. 68)
- 30 macaron shells (p. 108)
- strawberry jam (p. 113)

METHOD

1. Pipe the buttercream in an anticlockwise direction around the periphery of 15 macaron shells, leaving their centres empty.

2. Drop ½ a teaspoon of strawberry jam into the centre of each macaron. Put the empty shells on top of their filled partners and press down gently to make 15 macarons. Place in the fridge to set and then serve, preferably that day, but these will keep in an airtight container for 4 days.

raspberry singles

Vanilla **macaron shells** (p. 108) with pink **buttercream** (p. 68)
and **fresh raspberries**.

I like the idea of dessert being single,

just for me

Dessert has its place in a setting: sometimes it's there to be enjoyed and celebrated with family or friends, other times it's a singular, self-indulgent experience. I began to expand the concept I had developed for eeni mini cakes into ranges of mini individual desserts for all of my sweets — pushing boundaries and challenging the ways desserts had traditionally been created and served.

Layer five

ICE-CREAM JOURNEY

Contrast is a really beautiful tool in dessert design.
Being able to work with a few main colours
that complement each other, and using one or two
differing textures, can create something
that is pure magic.

in Layer five ...

EENI MINI ICE CREAMS

I love the idea of small desserts. They are easy to eat, elegant *and* inviting. And when grouped together, especially on a lovely serving tray, they can look so sophisticated and dainty.

Because I adore ice cream, I wanted to play with the idea of scale by taking something that's usually served in a large portion and shrinking it down to something really small, feminine and pretty.

Through this process, I made eeni mini ice-cream cakes as well as little waffle cones filled with chocolate, cake and buttercream or ganache. These are perfect little desserts for events and special occasions — a novelty idea that manages to retain all the class of a stylish and sophisticated dessert. It's sort of a modern play on having cake or chocolate fillings for a dessert event. I still make flavours for delicious cold ice creams and use those in the summer months, but I also want to show you how you can integrate ice-cream-style desserts into your celebrations in other ways.

MY FAVOURITE ICE CREAMS

These are four of my favourite flavours, but any of the syrups on pages 231–32 would also make great flavours for these ice creams.

MAKES: an ice-cream machine will yield about 7 large scoops, enough to fill 14 eeni mini ice creams

MIXING TIME: 25–30 minutes; FREEZING TIME: 4–5 hours

PEANUT BUTTER

INGREDIENTS
- 600 ml (21 fl oz) thickened (whipping) cream
- 310 ml (10¾ fl oz/1¼ cups) milk
- 220 g (7¾ oz/1 cup) caster (superfine) sugar
- 140 g (5 oz/½ cup) smooth peanut butter

LEMON

INGREDIENTS
- 600 ml (21 fl oz) thickened (whipping) cream
- 310 ml (10¾ fl oz/1¼ cups) milk
- 220 g (7¾ oz/1 cup) caster (superfine) sugar
- finely grated zest of 1 lemon
- 1 vanilla bean, split in half and seeds scraped out

VANILLA × RHUBARB

INGREDIENTS
- 600 ml (21 fl oz) thickened (whipping) cream
- 310 ml (10¾ fl oz/1¼ cups) milk
- 220 g (7¾ oz/1 cup) caster (superfine) sugar
- 1 vanilla bean, split in half and seeds scraped out (see note)
- ½ a batch rhubarb syrup (p. 232)

NOTE You only need the seeds from the vanilla bean for the ice cream. But the remaining pod is still full of vanilla flavour, so here are some ways you can make use of that: stick it in a jar of sugar to create vanilla-flavoured sugar, add to it to hot chocolates or warm milk to infuse flavour, use it as a decorative element for cakes or other desserts, or pop it in a bottle of vodka to create a delicious vanilla-infused cocktail.

If making lemon ice cream, start with step 2 below before proceeding with step 1.

1. Add all the ingredients to the bowl of a stand mixer and mix on a high speed until everything is combined and the mixture is nice and smooth. Spoon the mixture into an ice-cream machine (unless making the sugared apple, see below) and mix for 15–20 minutes, or according to manufacturer's instructions. Transfer the ice cream to a freezer-safe container and place plastic wrap on top of the container followed by a lid. Freeze for at least 4 hours before serving.

2. **Lemon ice cream:** In a saucepan, gently warm the milk with the lemon zest and the vanilla bean seeds and pod. Remove from the heat and allow to cool and infuse. Remove the vanilla pod before adding the mixture to the stand mixer with the rest of the ingredients.

SUGARED APPLE

INGREDIENTS
- 450 ml (16 fl oz) thick (double) cream
- 390 g (13¾ oz) condensed milk
- 1 teaspoon vanilla extract or paste
- 2 drops AmeriColor Soft Gel Paste in Dusty Rose
- a batch of sugared apple syrup (p. 233), without the fruit

METHOD
For this ice cream, follow step 1 above, but skip the ice-cream machine and go straight from the stand mixer to a freezer-safe container for 4–5 hours. You can replace the apple syrup with ½ a cup of caramel or strawberry syrup (see page 113), 4 tablespoons of smooth peanut butter or 2 capfuls of your favourite essence (such as vanilla or fairy floss [cotton candy]). Just be sure to taste after adding the first capful, as the flavours can be very concentrated.

PLAY WITH OTHER FLAVOUR COMBINATIONS

Caramel with popcorn, chocolate chip with peppermint essence, cookie and cream biscuits crushed up and stirred through before freezing, pink lemonade essence or elderflower syrup.

EENI MINI ICE CREAM DOUBLE SHOTS

MAKES: 30 mini ice creams

PREP TIME: 10 minutes

INGREDIENTS
- 30 mini waffle cones (see note below)
- 100 g (3½ oz) dark chocolate (70% cocoa)
- a batch of vanilla × rhubarb ice cream (p. 124)
- a batch of sugared apple ice cream (p. 125)
- sprinkles or crushed meringue (p. 56)

METHOD

1. Arrange the cones in a tray (see tip below) so they are easy to decorate. Melt the chocolate in the microwave in a heatproof bowl, in 30-second blasts, stirring until smooth and melted. Alternatively, place the chocolate in a heatproof bowl and sit over a bowl of simmering water, making sure the water doesn't touch the base of the bowl. Stir gently until smooth and melted.

2. Spoon a few teaspoons of ice cream, alternating between the flavours, into each cone. Working quickly, drizzle the melted chocolate over each cone and add a pinch of sprinkles before the chocolate sets. Place in the freezer until ready to serve.

NOTE The little waffle cones I use are just over 6 cm (2½ inches) long and 2.5 cm (1 inch) wide at the opening. They are available at specialty stores, online and in some good supermarkets. If you can't find ones this small, use larger cones, but bear in mind you won't get as many in a batch.

TIP Acrylic trays with small drilled holes are the perfect way to decorate, store and serve ice-cream cones. I like to have one tray in the freezer and the other on the bench while I decorate a few ice creams at a time, then I swap them over and keep the finished ones in the freezer until I'm ready to serve. Before you start assembling your ice creams, make sure you've cleared enough room in your freezer for two trays.

EENI MINI ROSETTE CONES

An indulgent combination of cupcake, chocolate and buttercream, this is a great dessert to serve at any celebration.

MAKES: 24 indulgent cones.

PREP TIME: 15 minutes MAKE TIME: 14 minutes

ASSEMBLY TIME: 15 minutes

YOU'LL NEED

- 100 g (3½ oz) dark chocolate (70% cocoa)
- 24 eeni mini waffle cones (see note on page 126)
- ½ a batch of eeni mini cupcakes (p. 67) (this will make 12 eeni mini cupcakes; enough for 24 cones)
- a batch of basic buttercream (p. 68) tinted with 1 small drop of AmeriColor Soft Gel Paste in Dusty Rose (or in varying shades of pink, as I've made here)
- piping (icing) bag with pipe tip 1M

METHOD

1. Melt the chocolate in 30-second blasts in a heatproof bowl in the microwave, stirring every 30 seconds until smooth and melted. Alternatively, place the chocolate in a heatproof bowl and sit it over a bowl of simmering water, making sure the water doesn't touch the base of the bowl. Stir gently until smooth and melted.

2. Arrange the cones in a tray for decorating (see tip on page 126).

3. Drizzle a small teaspoon of melted chocolate into each ice-cream cone. Cut the cooled cupcakes into halves or quarters (whichever fits easiest into your cones). Gently push a piece of cupcake into each cone, as far down as possible.

4. Put the buttercream in the piping bag and pipe buttercream rosettes into the cones (see caption below for instructions). Once piped, place in the fridge until serving so the chocolate can set.

NOTE If you like, you can use ice cream instead of buttercream for the rosettes. Just make sure the ice cream is fairly thick (not runny). Arrange the filled cones in the acrylic tray, pipe quickly and then freeze immediately.

When piping these rosettes, the piping bag should be positioned vertically above the centre of the cone and you should pipe with firm pressure. Rotate in an anticlockwise direction once. Repeat for each cone.

Take a sketch book somewhere relaxing and picturesque.
Start drawing what you see, but don't think too
much about it — keep to simple lines.
This process will help you start relaxing your mind
and get into the creative groove.

EENI MINI GANACHE TOP HATS

For these ganache top hats, make a batch of **chocolate ganache** (p. 113) and spoon it into a piping (icing) bag fitted with pipe tip 6B or 8B. Holding the piping bag vertically over the top of a **mini waffle cone** (see note page 126), use firm pressure to push the ganache into the cone till it reaches the top. Gently pull the piping bag up to release. Repeat until you have filled 24 mini cones. To finish them off, top each cone with a **macaron shell** (p. 108) or a **mini meringue** (p. 49) and/or an **edible rose pearl**.

Layer six

TART JOURNEY

*Nature is a beautiful teacher. She reminds us
that flowers bloom, in time*

in Layer six ...

THE CHALLENGING TART

From a really young age, I loved to peel and eat lemons with salt, an obsession that continues to this day — often when I discover a wedge floating in my mineral water at a restaurant.

This love of lemons runs in my family. I was in my early twenties when my sister made a lemon tart for me. For a first attempt, she did an incredible job. I remember it to this day because it opened my eyes to a different type of baking. Until then, I'd always seen tarts as savoury dishes, not desserts. This lemon tart also introduced me to the concept of making each element — base, filling, decorative top — completely from scratch. I was intrigued and saw endless possibilities ...

But I have to confess that tarts were *not* my favourite dessert to master. Shrinking, burning and breaking — perfecting that pastry shell was a real challenge — but the rewards in flavour and texture made it one worth conquering.

As with so many desserts, the biggest lesson learned when I began testing my tarts was to take the time to do each step properly. It's so important not to rush a process, and the more I started to accept this, the easier it became to master. So give yourself plenty of time for each stage, from making the pastry to filling and decorating. Working a day ahead will certainly ensure you end up with something really special to display and eat.

CONCEPT BUILDING
Mix-and-match Tarts

Always with a camera in hand, I like to capture moments and find inspiration in the outdoors and connect those things to my dessert work. A street full of interesting-looking buildings that contrast but complement each other sparked the idea for these mix-and-match tarts. They're perfect for special events or a casual lunch.

I LIKE TO THINK MAKING A TART IS LIKE CONSTRUCTING A BUILDING: a solid structure and a good foundation come first. Then there's the discovery of the inner layer. In a tart, this can be a surprising and indulgent mix of flavours, a merging of a gooey, soft filling with the light flaky pastry base. A few finishing touches enhance what's already there.

A SUCCESSFUL EXTERIOR IS CAREFULLY CONSIDERED. Things like gates, fences and paint colours add style and personality to the buildings they adorn. In tarts, I translate these elements into chocolate lines, delicate meringues or flourishes of piped ganache. I often look to flowers to create the last pretty details, similar to flower boxes or gardens. The last step is serving them in an unexpected way, by slicing them into bite-sized pieces and presenting them in an interesting arrangement — in a circle, or on serving boards. They make a pretty display and they go very quickly when placed on roaming trays.

MIX-AND-MATCH TARTS

TWO BASIC SWEET PASTRY RECIPES

Both of these simple pastries will make enough for six or seven small tarts, which you can blind bake ahead of time and store in an airtight container for a couple of days. Alternatively, you can freeze the dough for up to 1 month if it's wrapped really tightly in a couple of layers of plastic wrap. Allow it to thaw out overnight in the fridge before rolling out and baking.

MAKES: enough for 6 or 7 small 10 cm (4 inch) tarts
or one large 20 cm (8 inch) tart
PREP TIME: 15 minutes (plus chilling and rolling time)
BAKING TIME: 10–12 minutes

PLAIN PASTRY

INGREDIENTS

- 200 g (7 oz) unsalted butter, softened
- 120 g (4¼ oz) soft icing mixture or icing (confectioners') sugar
- 1½ eggs (see page 30)
- 1 teaspoon vanilla extract or essence (optional)
- 370 g (13 oz) plain (all-purpose) flour, plus extra for dusting
- canola oil cooking spray

CHOCOLATE PASTRY

INGREDIENTS

- 200 g (7 oz) unsalted butter softened
- 120 g (4½ oz) soft icing mixture or icing (confectioners') sugar
- 1½ eggs (see page 30)
- ½ egg yolk
- 370 g (13 oz) plain (all-purpose) flour, plus extra for dusting
- 60 g (2¼ oz) unsweetened cocoa powder
- pinch of sea or Himalayan salt
- canola oil cooking spray

EQUIPMENT

- electric kitchen scales
- measuring spoons
- stand mixer with paddle attachment
- good-quality plastic wrap
- good-quality baking paper
- rolling pin
- 6 or 7 tart tins 10 cm (4 inches) in diameter
- sharp knife
- scissors
- baking beads/uncooked rice or beans
- baking tray

METHOD

1. Place the softened butter in the bowl of a stand mixer and beat on a medium speed until creamy and soft.

2. Reduce the speed to low and slowly add the soft icing mixture a little at a time until completely incorporated.

3. For plain pastry, add the eggs and vanilla now. For chocolate pastry, add the eggs and egg yolk until fully mixed in.

4. Slowly add the flour. If making chocolate pastry, add the cocoa and salt now too. Mix until a dough has just started to form.

5. Transfer the dough from the stand mixer to a clean bench lightly dusted with flour and knead with clean, lightly floured hands for a few minutes until you have a smooth ball. Don't overwork the dough, just knead it enough to bring it together into that smooth ball. Cut the dough in half and then form each half into a ball again. Push down on each ball to create a disc, and then tightly wrap both discs in plastic wrap.

6. Chill the dough in the fridge for 2 hours. (You can leave it overnight if you are making this ahead of time.) The dough will need time to come to room temperature before you roll it out.

ROLLING OUT YOUR PASTRY

METHOD

1. Place one disc of dough between two sheets of baking paper (see p. 140) then begin to roll out to form a thin rectangle of pastry about 8 × 6 cm (3¼ × 2½ inches) and about 1 cm (½ inch) thick. Repeat with the other dough disc.

2. Lightly spray your tart tins with the canola oil.

3. Using a sharp knife, cut each rolled sheet of pastry into 6 pieces, each larger than a tart tin. That way, there will be overhanging pastry when you line the tins. Use your fingers to gently but firmly push the dough into the tart tin. If any area is short of pastry, add some dough so that it is covered. Repeat with the rest of the pastry and the tart tins.

4. Run your rolling pin over each tart tin so any overhanging pastry is trimmed off and you have a clean edge.

5. Poke a few holes in the base of each tart with a fork.

6. Cover the pastry-lined tins tightly with plastic wrap, then place the tins in the fridge and allow to chill for at least 3 hours, or overnight.

7. Preheat the oven to 170°C (325°F) fan-forced (FF).

8. Cut out six small squares of baking paper, each big enough to cover a tart tin.

9. Fill the lined tart tins with baking beads, then blind bake for 6 minutes.

10. Remove the baking paper and baking beads then return the tart shells to the oven for a further 10–12 minutes (or 7, if you are making frangipane tarts, see note below), until slightly golden, then allow to cool completely in their tins on a wire rack.

NOTE If making frangipane tarts, remove the tart shells from the oven after 7 minutes of extra baking time then follow the instructions on page 150.

PASTRY ROLLING

1. Roll the dough between two sheets of baking paper. Cut the pastry into six equal pieces.

2. Place a piece of pastry on top of a tart tin. Ensure there is an ample amount of pastry hanging over the sides of the tin. Press firmly but gently into the tin. Run the rolling pin over the top of the tin to cut off any excess dough.

3–4. Prick each pastry base with a fork to help ensure it cooks evenly.

5. Chill in the fridge for a few hours. This helps to prevent the pastry from shrinking when cooked.

6. Arrange on a baking tray. Line with baking paper then fill to the top with baking beads or uncooked rice or beans. Follow the instructions for baking on page 139.

TOP TIPS

- Take your time when making tarts.

- Allow enough time for the dough to chill and relax in the fridge before being rolled out — at least 2 hours.

- The tart shells need to chill again in the fridge after they have been rolled into their tins. Again, a few hours is best, as this will help prevent the dough from shrinking.

LEMON CURD

MAKES: 350 g (12 oz), enough to fill four small
10 cm (4 inches) tart shells

INGREDIENTS
- 2 eggs
- 2 egg yolks
- 150 g (5½ oz) caster (superfine) sugar
- finely grated zest of 1 lemon
- juice of 2 lemons
- 60 g (2¼ oz) chilled unsalted butter

METHOD
1. In a medium heavy-based saucepan over a low heat, whisk the eggs, egg yolks and sugar together until you have a smooth, thick consistency. You can remove the saucepan from the heat a couple of times as you whisk.

2. Add the lemon zest, juice and butter, and continue to whisk. This will take about 5 minutes over a low heat. Do not leave the saucepan unattended; you need to whisk continuously until the mixture thickens.

3. Remove from the heat and pass the lemon curd through a fine sieve over a bowl. If you decant it into a sterilised jar, this mixture will keep for about 2 weeks in the fridge.

*sharp and silky, smooth and bright,
sunshine yellow, you delight.*

CHOCOLATE ON CHOCOLATE

Spread a thin layer of **caramel** or **strawberry jam** or **peanut butter** around the base of a small **chocolate pastry tart shell** (p. 138). Fill a piping (icing) bag fitted with pipe tip 6B with **chocolate ganache** (p. 113) — one batch will fill two small tart shells. Holding the piping bag vertical to the tart and using firm pressure, work from the outside of the tart to the centre, piping little stars of ganache until the tart is completely filled. Finish with a tiny sprinkle of **sea salt**, and decorate with **edible flowers** such as miniature pansies. Serve with **vanilla ice cream**, if you like.

FRAÎCHE LEMON TARTS

Add 3 tablespoons of **crème fraîche** to half a batch of the **lemon curd** (p. 141) then use an electric mixer to whisk until combined. Fill four small **plain tart shells** (p. 138) with the mixture. Melt 20 g (¾ oz) of **dark chocolate** in a microwave in 30-second bursts. Dip a metal spatula into the melted chocolate then drizzle over the tarts and run a line through them to create pretty patterns. Shave a little **extra chocolate** on top, if you like. Finish with a few little squares of **salted caramel chocolate**, a dusting of **snow sugar** and some **white sprinkles**.

SALTED CARAMEL

MAKES: 300 g ($10\frac{1}{2}$ oz), enough to fill two small 10 cm (4 inch) tarts

PREP TIME: 10 minutes

INGREDIENTS

- 90 g (3¼ oz) unsalted butter
- 100 g (3½ oz) soft brown sugar
- 150 ml (5 fl oz) thickened (whipping) cream
- 1 tablespoon golden syrup or treacle

METHOD

1. Place all the ingredients in a heavy-based saucepan over a low heat.

2. Stir until the butter is melted and combined with the other ingredients.

3. Increase the heat to high and bring to the boil for 2 minutes. Remove from the heat, place in a clean bowl and allow to cool slightly before placing plastic wrap directly onto the caramel.

4. Chill in the fridge until set, for at least 3–4 hours, but overnight is best.

CRÈME PÂTISSIÈRE

MAKES: 300 g ($10\frac{1}{2}$ oz), enough to fill two small tarts

PREP TIME: 10 minutes

INGREDIENTS

- 200 ml (7 fl oz) milk
- 50 g (1¾ oz) caster (superfine) sugar
- 3 egg yolks
- 10 g (¼ oz) cornflour (cornstarch)
- 10 g (¼ oz) plain (all-purpose) flour
- finely grated zest of 1 lemon
- 1 teaspoon vanilla extract or essence

METHOD

1. Warm the milk and half of the sugar in a medium heavy-based saucepan over a low heat.

2. In a large bowl, whisk the egg yolks and the remaining sugar until they form a thick paste.

3. Slowly add the cornflour and plain flour to the egg mixture and continue to whisk until they are completely incorporated.

4. Using a large spoon, add some of the thick paste to the warm milk and begin to whisk — this is all done over a low heat to start with.

5. Add the remaining paste to the milk and continue to whisk. You can increase the heat to medium at this point, but do not leave unattended. Keep whisking until the mixture becomes thick. Add the lemon zest and vanilla to the mixture before removing from the heat.

6. Spoon the crème pâtissière into a clean bowl and allow to cool slightly before placing plastic wrap directly onto it. Cool completely in the fridge.

When making tarts, always think about flavours that contrast yet work well together. For example, dark chocolate, which is bitter, goes beautifully with sweet caramel. This combination is further enhanced by a hint of good-quality salt, such as Murray River, Maldon or pink Himalayan.

SALTED CARAMEL PRETZEL TART

Fill a small **chocolate pastry tart shell** (p. 138) with a few tablespoons of the **salted caramel filling** (p. 144) then use a knife or spoon to smooth it out. Melt 20 g (¾ oz) of **dark chocolate** in a small heatproof bowl in the microwave in 30-second blasts, stirring until smooth. Use a knife to create pretty drizzles of the melted chocolate on top of the caramel. Top with two **salted pretzels**, a pinch of **pink sprinkles** and **clear sugar sprinkles**, and a little pinch of **salt**.

SALTED CARAMEL AND DARK CHOCOLATE TART

Make two **salted caramel pretzel tarts** (opposite), but instead of adding pretzels and sprinkles, melt 100 g (3½ oz) of **dark chocolate** (70% cocoa) in a small heatproof bowl in the microwave in 30-second blasts. Smooth half of the melted chocolate over one tart, and half over the other. Carefully add a **small meringue wreath** (p. 61) as a garnish. It's nice to add the melted chocolate to the tart just before serving to guests so the chocolate is nice and oozy.

CRÈME PÂTISSIÈRE ×
RASPBERRY SNOW

Fill a small **plain pastry tart shell** (p. 138) with 1–2 tablespoons of **crème pâtissière** (p. 144) and level off with a spatula. Place a dozen or so **fresh raspberries** (the prettiest ones from the punnet) on top, then sprinkle over teaspoon of **snow sugar** to finish.

Every once in a while she would allow herself to wander through the city in search of

PINK
SKIES

FRANGIPANE DREAM

MAKES: enough filling for four small 10 cm (4 inch) tarts

PREP TIME: 10 minutes

INGREDIENTS

- 90 g (3¼ oz) unsalted butter, softened
- 100 g (3½ oz) caster (superfine) sugar, plus an extra teaspoon for decorating
- 2 eggs
- 90 g (3¼ oz) almond meal
- 15 g (½ oz) plain (all-purpose) flour
- 15 g (½ oz) soft icing mixture or icing (confectioners') sugar
- pinch of fine salt
- 4 small plain pastry tart shells (see recipe and note on p. 138)
- handful of frozen berries

METHOD

1. Beat the butter in the bowl of a stand mixer fitted with the paddle attachment over a medium speed until soft, then add the caster sugar and continue to beat until light and fluffy.

2. Add one egg at a time until fully incorporated.

3. Add all of the remaining ingredients except the frozen berries to the bowl and mix on high speed for 1–2 minutes.

4. Divide the mixture between the tart shells, and sprinkle some frozen berries into each shell. Push the berries down gently with your fingers so they are slightly submerged in the frangipane filling.

5. Bake for 4 minutes, then sprinkle the extra caster sugar on top of each tart. Return the tarts to the oven and bake for another 8–10 minutes, or until golden.

TIP   Allow the tarts to cool, then top with a few slices of fresh strawberry and some fresh blueberries. Add a pretty edible flower too, if you like.

Frangipane dream

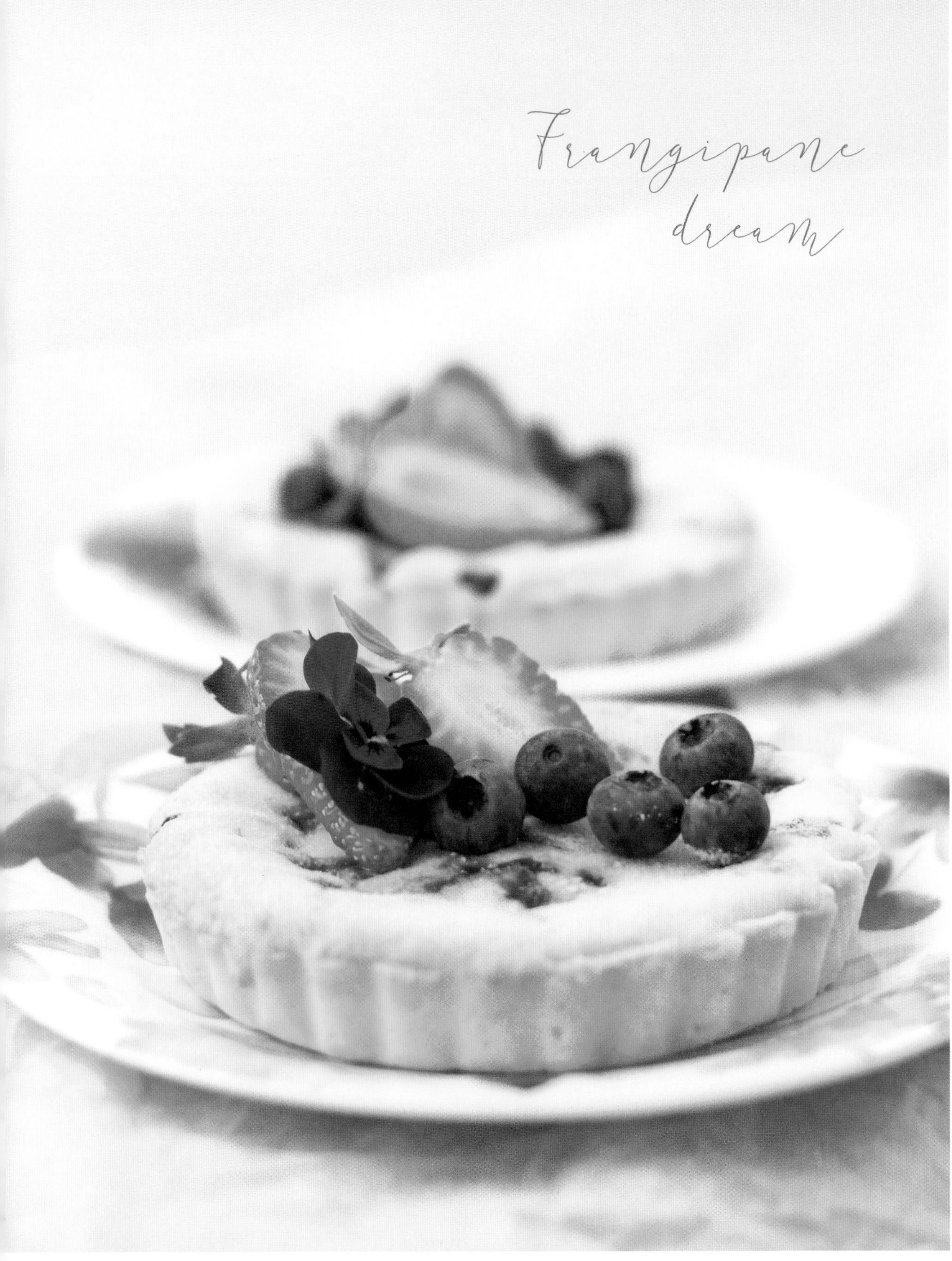

Layer seven

EENI MINI CAKE JOURNEY

And now, we eat cake

in Layer seven ...

SMALL BUT PERFECTLY FORMED

When I think of femininity, the words delicate, dainty, pretty
and petite spring to mind. After starting my business, I wanted
to create a range of cakes that were sophisticated but girly.
I thought a lot about what I found visually appealing, and kept
coming back to small and delicate — words not often associated
with cakes, where the trend has been 'bigger is better'.

My eeni mini cakes are small, stylish and easy to share between
a small group of friends. They are also a great size for ensuring no
food is wasted. There's no limit to the ways they can be decorated
and presented: a solitary cake for someone very special, or an army
of little cakes to create impact at a larger event ... they are the small
but perfect foundation for great memories.

take a chance

Go for a walk in the rain
and experience a few drops on your hands,

or, if you are daring enough,
on your face.

Sometimes letting everything go and allowing yourself to experience something for a moment can be enough to brighten your day and open your mind. I love having a few bright umbrellas at my front door for when I'm walking out in the rain — a pink umbrella feels so fun and uplifting against the grey.

BASIC VANILLA EENI MINI CAKE

MAKES: two 15 cm (6 inch) cakes

PREP TIME: 20 minutes BAKING TIME: 45–50 minutes

INGREDIENTS

- canola oil cooking spray
- 300 g (10½ oz/2 cups) plain (all-purpose) flour
- 50 g (1¾ oz) almond meal
- 3 teaspoons baking powder
- ½ teaspoon salt
- 225 g (8 oz) Nuttelex or unsalted butter, softened
- 350 g (12 oz) caster (superfine) sugar
- 4 eggs
- 1 teaspoon vanilla extract or essence (optional; see suggested flavours below for alternatives)
- food colouring (optional: 1–2 drops of AmeriColor Soft Gel Paste in Dusty Rose)
- 230 ml (7¾ fl oz) milk

EQUIPMENT

- good-quality baking paper
- pencil
- two 15 cm (6 inch) round cake tins
- scissors
- electric kitchen scales
- measuring spoons
- measuring cups
- sieve
- large mixing bowl
- stand mixer with whisk attachment
- small mixing bowl
- silicone spatula
- metal spatula
- 2 wire racks

SUGGESTED FLAVOURS

- finely grated zest of 1 lemon
- finely grated zest of 1 orange
- your choice of 8 mixed berries, push them into the cake batter once it's poured into the tin
- 1–2 tablespoons ground coffee or 1 teaspoon of freshly ground coffee (always start with 1 teaspoon first, then taste the flavour of the cake batter and build from there according to your flavour preference)
- 20 g (¾ oz) unsweetened cocoa powder (if using this, use 20 g less flour)
- 1 capful of strawberry essence
- 1–2 drops of fairy floss (cotton candy) essence or 1–2 drops of lemon essence (taste and add a drop or two more if needed)

When I'm lucky enough to have very fresh organic eggs from a farmers' market, their bright yolks often turn my vanilla cakes a wonderful shade of yellow.

Using a metal spatula and starting from the middle, rotate clockwise to smooth out the cake batter. This will help the cake to bake evenly.

METHOD

1. Preheat the oven to 170°C (325°F) fan forced (FF) and position one of the shelves in the middle of the oven.

2. Using your baking paper, pencil and tins, trace out two circles and cut them out. Also cut out two thick, long strips of baking paper for the sides of the tins.

3. Spray the tins lightly with canola oil then line both tins with the paper circles and strips.

4. Sift all the dry ingredients except the sugar into a large mixing bowl.

5. Beat the Nuttelex and sugar in a stand mixer on a high setting until the mixture is light, fluffy and pale.

6. Turn the speed down to low then add one egg at a time until fully incorporated.

7. In a small bowl, mix together the vanilla extract (or flavour of your choice), the food colouring, if using, and the milk.

8. Still on a low speed, alternate between adding the sifted dry ingredients and the milk mixture until just incorporated. Do not overbeat the mixture.

9. Place a lined baking tin onto the scales and ensure the scales are zeroed. You are going to weigh out 650 g (1 lb 7 oz) of cake batter for each tin.

10. Smooth out the cake batter using a metal spatula, starting in the middle of the tin and moving the spatula in a clockwise direction.

11. Place the cake tins on the middle shelf in the oven, and bake for 45 minutes. Check after 40 minutes, inserting a skewer tilted at a slight angle into the centre of the cake. If it comes out clean, the cakes are ready. If not, bake for an extra 5 minutes.

12. Allow the cakes to cool for 10 minutes in their tins before transferring to wire racks to cool completely.

FILLING AND STACKING A CAKE

1

2

3

4

5

1. Use a serrated knife or cake leveller to trim the top off each cake evenly.

2. Using a piping (icing) bag with piping tip 1A, create a spiral of buttercream in the middle of each layer. Do three rotations, and then stop.

3. Using a small spatula, smooth out the icing out evenly. Carefully stack the next cake on top, press down gently and repeat.

4. Once you've finished filling and stacking your cake, create the crumb coat — the thin layer of icing all over the cake. This acts as a base for the decorative icing later. A rectangular cake scraper and a turntable will help you rotate the cake in one direction while you smooth in the other. Smooth the side and top of the cake. Keep a small bowl near you so you can add or remove any excess icing as you go.

5. Chill the cake for at least 1 hour (4 hours, if you can) so the crumb coat sets before you proceed to decorating. This will allow you to get a much cleaner finish. Make sure your cake is on a cake board at this point.

SMOOTH ICED CAKE

1. Remove the chilled crumb-coated cake (see opposite) from the fridge and place on a cake turntable to decorate.

2. Add a couple of spoonfuls of icing to the top and side of the cake.

3. Using a flat cake spatula, begin rotating the cake anticlockwise while moving your spatula clockwise, smoothing out the icing thinly as you go to cover the cake.

4. Continue to add icing where needed until your cake has is completely covered in a thin layer of icing.

5. Smooth out any lumps and remove any excess icing to a bowl. The top of the cake will have some excess icing. To smooth this out, you will need to drag the icing in towards the centre of the cake using your spatula.

STRAWBERRY AND CHOCOLATE DELIGHT

MAKES: two 15 cm (6 inch) cakes

PREP TIME: 20 minutes BAKING TIME: 45–50 minutes

INGREDIENTS
- 1 batch of basic eeni mini cake batter (p. 158)
- 20 g (¾ oz) unsweetened cocoa powder
- 1 capful of strawberry essence
- AmeriColor Soft Gel Paste in Red Red

METHOD
Make the cake batter, but leave out the vanilla flavouring. Line two cake tins and set them aside. Divide the cake batter evenly between two mixing bowls by weighing 650 g/1 lb 7 oz into each one. Add the cocoa powder to one of the bowls, and mix in well. Add the strawberry essence and a drop of red food colouring to the other. Mix in well then spoon the chocolate batter into one tin, and the strawberry batter into the other. Level the batter and cook the cakes as on page 159. Allow to cool completely before decorating.

DECORATING THE CAKE

INGREDIENTS
- 1 batch of buttercream (p. 68)
- AmeriColor Soft Gel Paste in Red Red
- 1 capful of strawberry essence
- sugar sand
- 100 g (3½ oz) dark chocolate (70% cocoa), roughly chopped
- piping (icing) bag with rose pipe tip 1M

METHOD
1. Put a third of the buttercream in a clean bowl and leave it uncoloured — this will be for the top and side of the cake. Slowly add a couple of drops of red food colouring to the remaining two-thirds of buttercream until you reach the desired shade. Add the strawberry essence to the red buttercream and beat in well. This will be used for the middle layer of filling, and for finishing off the top of the cake.

2. Neatly halve the chocolate cake horizontally. Smear a thin layer of red buttercream on top of one of the halves, then place the strawberry cake on top. Smear another layer of red buttercream on top of the strawberry cake, and top with the remaining chocolate cake layer, smoothest side facing up. Smear a thin layer of plain buttercream all over the top and around the side of the cake, then chill in the fridge for 1 hour before you finish decorating.

3. Finish the decorating with the sugar sand and pieces of chocolate. Put the remaining pink buttercream into a piping bag with a rose pipe tip and pipe pretty lines of icing with your hand tilted at a 60 degree angle.

Cascading Roses

MAKE IT EASY FOR YOURSELF

Good-quality baking paper makes a difference
to the end result.

•

If you're using reusable piping (icing) bags, wash them
then place them in the oven at 60°C (140°F) to dry them
for 5–6 minutes before putting them away.

•

Use canola oil cooking spray to grease all baking tins
before lining them with baking paper

•

Preheat your oven before you start measuring out
your ingredients, and check the oven's temperature
using an independent oven thermometer.

•

Always pay attention to ingredient expiry dates,
especially on things like baking powder, spices,
eggs and milk.

•

If you're baking a cake for an event or special occasion,
try to give yourself a trial run first. If you can't do that,
keep things as simple as possible.

•

Always place your lined cake tin on the scales, zero out
and then add the cake batter. This will ensure you always
get cakes of the same size.

MASTERING THE PRINCIPLE OF 'LESS IS MORE'

WILL HELP YOU TO START

PERFECTING YOUR TECHNIQUE

BECAUSE THERE WILL BE NOTHING TO HIDE BEHIND

BASIC PIPE TIPS

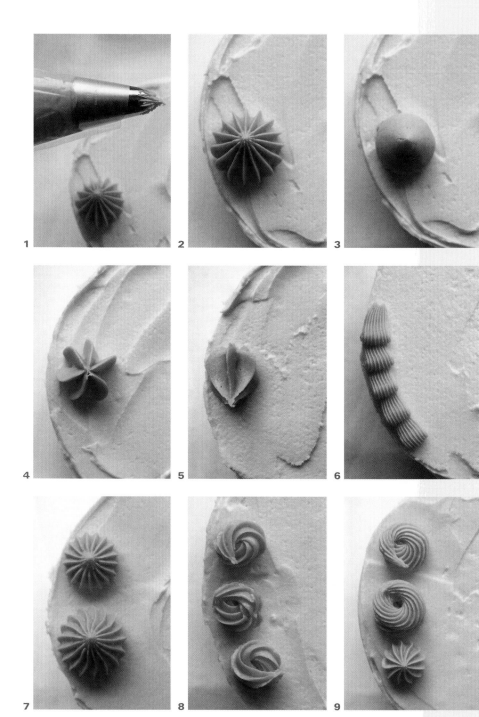

1–2 6B

3 1A

4 1M

5 1M piped at a
45-degree angle

6 48 piped at a
45-degree angle

7 8B (different levels of
pressure will give you
different sizes)

8 17 piped in an
anticlockwise rotation

9 22 downward star
(open star pipe tip) or
piped using anticlockwise
rotation on top of itself
twice

Tip

I have mainly used Wilton
pipe tips in this book
because they have a great
range and I'm comfortable
using them. That said, there
are lots of exciting pipe tips
in cake-decorating shops,
so experiment with any that
catch your eye and use
whatever feels right for you.

IMAGINE

EXPLORE

DESIGN

CREATE

COLLECT

OBSERVE

MASTER

CHALLENGE

STYLE

FEEL

EXPERIENCE

1

2

3

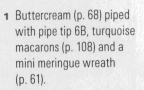

4

5

6

1 Buttercream (p. 68) piped with pipe tip 6B, turquoise macarons (p. 108) and a mini meringue wreath (p. 61).

2 Buttercream roses (pipe tip 1M), piped in an anticlockwise direction without stopping, three or four times on one side of the cake.

3 Three macarons (p. 108) filled with buttercream piped using pipe tip 6B.

4 A 15 cm (6 inch) tin meringue wreath (p. 61) piped using pipe tip 1M.

5 Buttercream piped with pipe tip 6B. Crushed meringue (p. 49) sprinkled over the cake to finish.

6 A 15 cm (6 inch) meringue wreath (p. 61) made using the basic meringue split into thirds, two of the thirds tinted with pink and darker pink. Piped using pipe tips 6B, 1A and 1M.

CONCEPT BUILDING

Same but Different:
Desert Rose and Cascading Roses

*A trip to LA was the perfect inspiration for dessert land,
with cactuses for miles and turquoise morning skies.
Using a strong base colour and a flawless icing look,
I created Desert Rose and Cascading Roses, two cakes that
share the same DNA but have very different personalities.*

BOTH CAKES USE the basic eeni mini cake batter (p. 158) and basic buttercream (p. 68) tinted with a few drops of AmeriColor in Turquoise. Save a couple of dessertspoons of buttercream for decorating and tint it with a few drops of Dusty Rose. The smooth iced technique (p. 161) will provide a smooth silhouette.

FOR MY DESERT ROSE CAKE I used pipe tip 6B to add a few interesting buttercream blooms around the perimeter. These echo some of the incredible desert flowers I saw. I wanted a more playful look that tied in to my original inspiration, so I finished this look with a cute cactus cookie (glued to the cake using some buttercream), pretty sprinkles and pink sugar sand.

THE CASCADING ROSES CAKE (p. 164) takes a more classic approach. I used pipe tip 1M to create the cluster of roses spilling over the side of the cake and finished with a sprinkle of clear sugar sand.

DESERT ROSE

A recent trim of the these lavender hedges was a wonderful reminder of how a few round shapes grouped together can make an arresting pattern. I used this image as part of my mood board when creating the 'Same but Different' eeni mini cakes on page 172.

Rooftop love

*A drive into an industrial area
led me to this large prickly pear
happily settled on a balcony.
Its beautiful shape and colour
provide a perfect example of
minimalism done well.*

SIMPLE ICED CAKE

The simply iced cake is not completely smoothed out; it's a little rough, giving it a rustic and romantic feel.

Before you start, make sure your cake and the filling inside it has had adequate time to chill in the fridge. Don't rush this process: give it at least 4 hours if you can. This allows the crumb coat and the filling inside to set, and prevents the layers of cake from sliding around. It also means that when the decorative icing comes into contact with the cake, it will set much quicker, giving you a cleaner result. Apply the icing liberally, and if you have a turntable, use it so that you're constantly rotating the cake while your hand is holding the spatula and smoothing out the icing.

Note
This style is not about smoothing and perfecting, it's about developing a slightly rough look.

SIMPLE ROUGHLY ICED CAKE

This is my favourite (and signature) cake design. The trick to achieving it is to use the simple iced cake as a base. Once the icing has been applied, move your spatula up or down, or back and forth on the cake to create a rough, wavy look. Typically, I find that my hand goes in a downward motion so that after I've moved the icing down, I move my spatula away from the cake, place it next to the wave I've just made and repeat the process.

I suggest practising by buying a chocolate spread you'd use on bread, and placing a large spoonful on a slice of bread. Slide your spatula back and forth over it to get a feel for the motion, and also the look.

RENDERED PINK BIRTHDAY CAKE

CONCEPT BUILDING
Rendered Pink Birthday Cake

A stroll to my local shops provided the perfect inspiration for this birthday cake. Flowers in bundles and a two-tone building provided the basis for this idea.

I STARTED WITH three 15 cm (6 inch) cakes: two vanilla (p. 158) and one strawberry (made by halving the recipe on page 162). I used buttercream (p. 68) for filling the cake and for the thin crumb coat around the outside. After chilling the cake for 4 hours, I decorated ...

I ROUGHLY ICED the cake all over (p. 177) with a fresh batch of buttercream that I'd tinted with a dusty rose colour. I reserved a little of this for piping later, then tinted the remaining buttercream with deeper shades of pink. By using a spatula to 'paint' on these deep pinks, I added colour and dimension to the cake. After topping with some sprinkles, I used pipe tip 6B for the rose-coloured buttercream swirls. Some gold leaf and a mini birthday hat provided the finishing touches.

The finish is all about the finer details:
sanding sugars, sprinkles and gold leaf can transform
a simple cake into something unique and special.

Sunny days, sandy toes.
Simple and adored.

Flower me pretty

Styling with flowers

The flavour of this cake is strawberry and lemon (see suggested flavours on page 158). I added one large drop of AmeriColor Soft Gel Paste in Deep Pink to the basic buttercream recipe (p. 68) and created some texture on the icing by tilting my spatula on a slight angle, repeating the process on half of the previous smear.

The colours of the flowers tie in to the fresh flavours used, and I stuck with only a few shades of a few different colours: green, white and yellow. After wrapping their stems tightly with florist tape, I inserted them carefully into the cake. A sprinkle of crushed meringue (p. 49) and clear sugar sand finishes the look.

Layer eight

CELEBRATION CAKE JOURNEY

Minimalism. Keep it simple.

in Layer eight ...

THE STATEMENT CAKES

As I drove through the stunning mountains of California, I was swept away by the beauty of the land. Shapes, colours and textures all seemed to work so seamlessly together. In the distance, cows grazed peacefully on grass, surrounded by what felt like eternal silence — no one around. The lines of the mountains, so cleanly outlined against the sky, had such power that I felt inspired to create designs that were clean but larger than my other desserts, and with greater presence.

For me, this photograph says so much about mastering the larger foundations while capturing the small and intricate details, and how grand scale can create an impressive backdrop for the finer elements. When I design and create celebration cakes, they need to have a much bolder impact, yet retain the simplicity and subtle detail I love. The basic techniques in this chapter need to be executed more carefully than in my eeni mini cakes due to the large size of the cake — which means any mistake will be noticed. They also need to have balanced flavours that work with the size of the cake, so as not to get lost.

The best advice I can give you before embarking on this particular cake journey is to give yourself several days to bring it together, two if you are short of time. Aim to do all the baking as well as piping the inner layers of icing on day one. The next day, decorate the outside of the cake. Add any final touches that may be vulnerable (such as flowers) right before presenting the cake, so it looks its absolute best.

CONCEPT BUILDING

Chocolate Tower

*You will be surprised by how much inspiration you can
get from going on a simple drive into a city and exploring.
I often prefer it if someone else does the driving
so I can take photos with my camera or phone. I love
looking at the different sizes and shapes of buildings,
and thinking about how my different pipe tips can
be used to build similar designs.*

HERE, THE DARK BROWNS AND BLACKS of the voids in the buildings
were the starting point for the rich Chocolate Tower cake (p. 190). The
multiple floors of the high-rise building inspired the many tiers of this
cake, each of which is clearly visible rather than iced over.

*Building the
layers of
thought in
a cake*

CHOCOLATE TOWER

CHOCOLATE TOWER

To make it easy, the recipe has been broken down
so that you can batch-make the number of cakes required
for this design. Make all of the cakes and cool them completely
before progressing to the decorating stage.

MAKES: two 15 cm (6 inch) round cakes and three 20 cm (8 inch) cakes

PREP TIME: 30 minutes BAKING TIME: 45–55 minutes

INGREDIENTS FOR ONE 15 CM (6 INCH) AND
ONE 20 CM (8 INCH) CAKE (BATTER A)
You will need to make this recipe twice
- canola oil cooking spray
- 210 g (7½ oz) self-raising flour
- 30 g (1 oz) almond meal
- 90 g (3¼ oz) unsweetened cocoa powder
- 1½ teaspoons bicarbonate of soda (baking soda)
- 150 g (5½ oz) good-quality dark chocolate (70% cocoa), grated
- 190 g (6¾ oz) unsalted butter, softened
- 165 g (5¾ oz) caster (superfine) sugar
- 3 eggs
- 1½ teaspoons vanilla extract or essence
- 120 g (4¼ oz) strawberry jam
- 375 ml (13 fl oz/1½ cups) milk

INGREDIENTS FOR ONE 8 INCH (20 CM) CAKE (BATTER B)
- 140 g (5 oz) self-raising flour
- 20 g (¾ oz) almond meal
- 60 g (2¼ oz) unsweetened cocoa powder
- 1 teaspoon bicarbonate of soda (baking soda)
- 100 g (3½ oz) good-quality dark chocolate (70% cocoa), grated
- 125 g (4½ oz/½ cup) unsalted butter, softened
- 110 g (3¾ oz/½ cup) caster (superfine) sugar
- 2 eggs
- 1 teaspoon vanilla extract or essence
- 80 g (2¾ oz) strawberry jam
- 250 ml (9 fl oz/1 cup) milk

EQUIPMENT

- good-quality baking paper
- pencil
- 15 cm (6 inch) cake tin
- two 20 cm (8 inch) cake tins
- scissors
- electric kitchen scales
- measuring spoons
- measuring cups
- sieve
- 2 large mixing bowls
- fine grater for chocolate
- stand mixer with whisk attachment
- silicone spatula
- 2 wire racks
- serrated knife or cake leveller
- 20 cm (8 inch) cake board
- 15 cm (6 inch) cake board (optional)
- piping (icing) bag and piping tip size 1M

METHOD

1. Preheat the oven to 170°C (325°F) fan-forced (FF).

2. Using baking paper, a pencil and your cake tins, trace five circles (two 15 cm and three 20 cm) and cut them out. Also cut out five thick, long strips of baking paper to line the sides of the tins.

3. Spray the cake tins with canola oil, then line them with the paper circles and strips.

4. Weigh out all of the ingredients for your cakes but keep the batters separate from each other. Start by making Batter A, then repeat until all of the cakes are baked. Sift all the dry ingredients except the sugar into a large mixing bowl and sprinkle in the grated dark chocolate. Mix together, then set aside.

5. In the bowl of a stand mixer, cream the butter and sugar together on a high speed until light and fluffy.

6. Reduce the mixer speed to medium and add one egg at a time until fully incorporated, then add the vanilla extract and the strawberry jam. Once well mixed, spoon into a large bowl.

7. Slowly fold the sifted dry ingredients and milk into the egg mixture, alternating between them, until everything is just combined.

8. Place a lined tin on the electric scale, zero it, then spoon in the batter. A 15 cm (6 inch) cake will need 600 g (1 lb 5 oz) of batter and a 20 cm (8 inch) cake will need 800 g (1 lb 12 oz).

9. Bake together: 45 minutes for a small cake and 55 minutes for a large one. Insert a skewer at a slight angle into the centre of each cake, if it comes out clean, the cake is ready. If not, cook for a few more minutes and check again.

NOTE When weighing the batters, always ensure you place the lined empty cake tin on the scales before zeroing. You'll need to change this for different-sized empty tins.

DECORATING

INGREDIENTS
- a double batch of basic buttercream (p. 68) (see step 1 below)
- 2–3 capfuls of strawberry essence
- 1 large drop of AmeriColor Soft Gel Paste in Fuchsia
  (or any other shade of pink)

METHOD

1. Follow the buttercream recipe on page 68 but replace the vanilla essence with a couple of drops of strawberry essence. Taste after adding each drop, as it can be a strong flavour.

2. Mix the food colouring into the buttercream until well incorporated and your desired shade of pink.

3. Place the buttercream in a piping (icing) bag fitted with pipe tip 1M and pipe a few small stars onto the 20 cm (8 inch) cake board, these will help to anchor your cake to the board.

4. Place one of your 20 cm cakes on the cake board, push down gently but firmly to secure it, then begin piping pink stars side by side (see image on page 184) until you have covered the entire top of the cake.

5. Carefully place the second 20 cm cake on top of the stars, then repeat the process.

6. When you come to stack the third 20 cm cake, ensure that the bottom of that cake is facing up — it's the smoothest and prettiest of the two sides. You won't need to pipe stars over the whole surface, only in the middle where your 15 cm (6 inch) cake will be sitting. If you need to, place a 15 cm tin onto the cake and use a knife to score around the shape to guide you — this really helps for accuracy.

7. Once you have piped stars the same diameter as the 15 cm cake, place one of the smaller cakes on top of the stars (you can place it on a board before doing this, if you like), then cover the top of that cake with piped stars, as before.

8. When placing the final small cake on top — ensure that the bottom of the cake is facing up. Pipe the stars on top.

9. To finish, decorate around the join of the two cake sizes with small rosettes piped in an anticlockwise direction. You can use the same pipe tip or a smaller one, such as pipe tip 17, if you wish.

Orange
Bloom

Going against the grain, photographing from angles, observing small details, learning simple techniques to build on the bigger ones. All these things create maps that continue to inspire and generate new ideas.

Nature

provides some of the most
powerful colours and moments of
inspiration. Take the time to capture
these things; photograph them
and make a note of how you feel
when you see such beauty.

I love to take pictures at different times
of the day because this helps me to
better understand lighting and capture
different colours and moods.

ORANGE BLOOM

MAKES: two 15 cm (6 inch) and three 20 cm (8 inch) cakes

PREP TIME: 30 minutes BAKING TIME: 45–50 minutes

INGREDIENTS FOR TWO 15 CM (6 INCH) CAKES (BATTER A)

- canola oil cooking spray
- 450 g (1 lb) caster (superfine) sugar
- 315 g (11 oz) self-raising flour
- 45 g (1¾ oz) almond meal
- 1½ teaspoons baking powder
- 120 g (4¼ oz) Nuttelex or unsalted butter, softened
- 4½ eggs (see page 30)
- finely grated zest of 1½ oranges
- 75 ml (2½ fl oz/⅓ cup) freshly squeezed orange juice
- 75 ml (2½ fl oz/⅓ cup) vegetable oil

INGREDIENTS FOR ONE 8 INCH (20 CM) CAKE (BATTER B)

- 300 g (10½ oz) caster (superfine) sugar
- 210 g (7½ oz) self-raising flour
- 30 g (1 oz) almond meal
- 1 teaspoon baking powder
- 80 g (2¾ oz) Nuttelex or unsalted butter, softened
- 3 eggs
- finely grated zest of 1½ oranges
- 50 ml (1½ fl oz) freshly squeezed orange juice
- 50 ml (1½ fl oz) vegetable oil

INGREDIENTS FOR TWO 8 INCH (20 CM) CAKES (BATTER C)

- 600 g (1 lb 5 oz) caster (superfine) sugar
- 420 g (15 oz) self-raising flour
- 60 g (2¼ oz) almond meal
- 2 teaspoons baking powder
- 160 g (5¾ oz) Nuttelex or unsalted butter, softened
- 6 eggs
- finely grated zest of 2 oranges
- 100 ml (3½ fl oz) freshly squeezed orange juice
- 100 ml (3½ fl oz) vegetable oil

EQUIPMENT

- pencil
- good-quality baking paper
- two 15 cm (6 inch) cake tins
- three 20 cm (8 inch) cake tins
- scissors
- silicone spatula
- 2 wire racks
- electric kitchen scales
- measuring cups and spoons
- measuring jug
- sieve
- large mixing bowl
- metal spatula
- stand mixer with whisk attachment
- sharp knife
- fine grater for zesting
- citrus juicer
- piping (icing) bag with round large piping tip size 1A
- serrated knife or cake leveller
- 2 cake boards: one 15 cm and one 20 cm

METHOD

1. Use a pencil to trace around your baking tins on the baking paper, then cut out five circles (two 15 cm and three 20 cm) as well as five long, thick strips to line the sides of the tins with. Spray the tins with canola oil then line the tins with the circles and strips.

2. Preheat the oven to 180°C (350°F) (FF).

3. Weigh out all of the ingredients for your cakes but keep the three batters separate from each other. Start by making Batter A, then repeat until all of the cakes are baked. Sift all of the dry ingredients into the bowl of a stand mixer.

4. Add all of the wet ingredients and then, on a medium speed with whisk attachment, beat the ingredients for 3 minutes.

5. Place one of your lined tins on the electric scales, zero out the scales and then weigh the cake batter (see note below).

6. Bake for 40–45 minutes for the smaller cakes, and 45–50 minutes for the large cakes. The baking times will vary based on how many cake tins you have in the oven, so always wait until 40 minutes have passed before you test a cake. Insert a skewer at a slight angle into the centre of each cake, if it comes out clean, the cake is ready. If not, cook for a few more minutes and check again.

7. Remove the cakes from the oven and leave to cool in the tins for 10 minutes before transferring to wire racks to cool completely.

8. Let the cakes cool for at least 2 hours before you start any decorating.

NOTE Add 650 g (1 lb 7 oz) of batter to a 15 cm (6 inch) tin and 850 g (1 lb 14 oz) to a 20 cm (8 inch) tin.

Lemon offers a wonderful fresh flavour to cakes and balances out their sweetness at the same time.

LEMON AND COCONUT DREAM

MAKES: two 15 cm (6 inch) cakes and three 20 cm (8 inch) cakes
(serves 40–50 people)

PREP TIME: 30 minutes   BAKING TIME: 45–50 minutes

DECORATING AND SETTING TIME: 4 hours

INGREDIENTS FOR TWO 15 CM (6 INCH) CAKES (BATTER A)
- canola oil cooking spray
- 300 g (10½ oz/2 cups) plain (all-purpose) flour
- 50 g (1¾ oz) almond meal
- 3 teaspoons baking powder
- ½ teaspoon fine salt (optional)
- 30 g (1 oz) desiccated (finely shredded) coconut
- 225 g (8 oz) Nuttelex or unsalted butter, softened
- 320 g (11¼ oz) caster (superfine) sugar
- 4 eggs
- 1½ teaspoons coconut essence
- finely grated zest of 1 lemon
- 230 ml (7¾ fl oz) milk

INGREDIENTS FOR TWO 20 CM (8 INCH) CAKES (BATTER B)
- 450 g (1 lb/3 cups) plain (all-purpose) flour
- 75 g (2¾ oz) almond meal
- 4½ teaspoons baking powder
- ½ teaspoon fine salt (optional)
- 45 g (1¾ oz) desiccated (finely shredded) coconut
- 340 g (11¾ oz) Nuttelex or unsalted butter, softened
- 480 g (1 lb 1 oz) caster (superfine) sugar
- 6 eggs
- 2 teaspoons coconut essence
- finely grated zest of 1½ lemons
- 350 ml (12 fl oz) milk

INGREDIENTS FOR ONE 20 CM (8 INCH) CAKE (BATTER C)
- 225 g (8 oz) plain (all-purpose) flour
- 40 g (1½ oz) almond meal
- 2¼ teaspoons baking powder
- a pinch of fine salt (optional)
- 20 g (¾ oz) desiccated (finely shredded) coconut
- 170 g (6 oz) Nuttelex or unsalted butter, softened
- 210 g (7½ oz) caster (superfine) sugar
- 3 eggs
- 1 teaspoon coconut essence
- finely grated zest of 1 lemon
- 170 ml (5½ fl oz/⅔ cup) milk

EQUIPMENT

- pencil
- two 15 cm (6 inch) cake tins
- three 20 cm (8 inch) cake tins
- good-quality baking paper
- scissors
- electric kitchen scales
- measuring spoons
- measuring jug
- sieve
- large mixing bowl
- silicone spatula
- stand mixer with whisk attachment
- fine zester for lemon
- metal spatula
- sharp knife
- piping (icing) bag with round large piping tip size 1A
- serrated knife or cake leveller
- 2 cake boards: one 15 cm (6 inch) and one 20 cm (8 inch)

METHOD

1. Preheat the oven to 170°C (325°F) (FF).

2. Use a pencil to trace around your baking tins on the baking paper, then cut out five circles (two 15 cm and three 20 cm) as well as five long, thick strips to line the sides of the tins with. Spray the tins with canola oil then line the tins with the circles and strips.

3. Weigh out all of the ingredients for your cakes but keep the three batters separate from each other. Start by making Batter A, then repeat until all of the cakes are baked. Sift the flour, almond meal, baking powder and salt into a large mixing bowl. Add the desiccated coconut, then mix together.

4. In the bowl of your stand mixer, beat the Nuttelex (or butter) and sugar together on low, increasing to high speed, until the mixture is light and fluffy.

5. Turn the speed to low then add one egg at a time, adding the next once the previous one is fully incorporated.

6. Add the coconut essence and lemon zest to the milk in a small bowl.

7. On a low speed, alternate between adding the sifted dry ingredients and the milk mixture. Do not overbeat the mixture.

8. Place the lined cake tins, one at a time, on the scales and ensure the scales are zeroed. Divide the cake batter between the tins (see note on page 199 for the weights).

9. Smooth out the cake batter using a metal spatula, moving from the middle of the tin in a clockwise direction (see p. 159).

10. Bake on the middle rack of the oven for 45 minutes (for the 15 cm cakes) and 50 minutes (for the 20 cm cakes). Check to see if they are cooked by inserting a skewer on an angle in the centre of each cake. If it comes out clean, they are cooked, if not, they may need a few minutes more.

11. Once cooked, allow the cakes to cool in their tins for 10 minutes before removing and cooling completely on a wire rack.

ICING AND DECORATING THE CAKE

PREP TIME: 1 hour

LEMON BUTTERCREAM FILLING

INGREDIENTS
- finely grated zest of 1 lemon
- juice of 1 lemon (optional)
- 2 capfuls of coconut essence
- double batch of basic buttercream (p. 68, omit the vanilla flavouring)

METHOD
1. Beat the lemon zest, juice (if you want it extra lemony) and coconut essence into the buttercream, a little at a time. Taste the buttercream after adding the juice and the first capful of coconut essence, to make sure the flavour isn't too strong. Add more if needed.

2. Stack and fill the large and small cakes with the lemon buttercream following the instructions on page 160. Once stacked, smear a thin layer or crumb coating around the outside and top of each cake. Once done, chill the cakes for at least 30 minutes in the fridge — 4 hours, if possible.

WHITE FROSTING

INGREDIENTS
- 250 g (9 oz) Solite Creaming Shortening (vegetable) (see page 31), at room temperature
- 500 g (1 lb 2 oz) pure icing (confectioners') sugar, sifted
- 125 ml (4 fl oz/½ cup) water
- 2 handfuls edible rose petals, frozen (see page 31)

METHOD
1. Place the Solite, icing sugar and the water in the bowl of a stand mixer. Beat with a whisk attachment until the ingredients are well combined. Turn the mixer up to high speed and beat for 5 minutes, until the frosting has doubled in volume.

2. Working with the larger cake first, spoon a generous amount of white frosting on the top and side of the cake. Use a flat spatula to smooth the cake in a clockwise direction while you rotate it anticlockwise. Continue adding frosting wherever it is needed until there is a thin layer completely covering the cake. Follow the smooth icing technique on page 161.

3. Use the flat spatula to smooth out any lumps. Remove any excess icing to a bowl as you go. To smooth out the top, drag the spatula towards the centre.

4. Repeat the process with the smaller cake, then follow the steps opposite to stack the cakes and apply the finishing touches.

STACKING AND FINAL TOUCHES

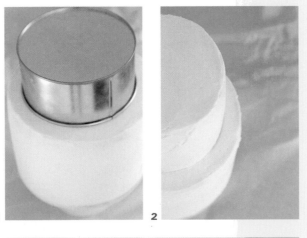

1

2

3

1 Use a clean cake tin the same size of the smaller cake to mark out where the smaller cake needs to be placed. This ensures it will be centred when you stack it on top.

2 Hold the iced smaller cake on either side and place gently within the cake tin marks.

3 You can leave the join of the two cakes exposed, or you can put some of the frosting in a piping bag (I've used pipe tip 17) and pipe a line of frosting around the join to hide it. Add handfuls of edible frozen rose petals to the cake and serve straight away.

Carrot
Celebration

CARROT CELEBRATION

MAKES: two 18 cm (7 inch) cakes and two 20 cm (8 inch) cakes
(serves 50–60 people)

PREP TIME: 30 minutes BAKING TIME: 50–60 minutes

INGREDIENTS FOR TWO 18 CM (7 INCH) CAKES (BATTER A)
- canola oil cooking spray
- 185 g (6½ oz) self-raising flour
- 185 g (6½ oz) plain (all purpose) flour
- 1½ teaspoons ground cinnamon
- 1½ teaspoons bicarbonate of soda (baking soda)
- ¾ teaspoon ground ginger
- 225 g (8 oz) soft brown sugar
- 6 eggs
- 325 ml (11 fl oz) olive oil
- 225 g (8 oz) golden syrup or treacle
- 450 g (1 lb) grated carrot (approximately 5 carrots)
- 90 g (3¼ oz) chopped walnuts

INGREDIENTS FOR TWO 20 CM (8 INCH) CAKES (BATTER B)
- 250 g (9 oz) self-raising flour
- 250 g (9 oz) plain (all-purpose) flour
- 2 teaspoons ground cinnamon
- 2 teaspoons bicarbonate of soda (baking soda)
- 1 teaspoon ground ginger
- 300 g (10½ oz) soft brown sugar
- 8 eggs
- 500 ml (17 fl oz/2 cups) olive oil
- 500 g (1 lb 2 oz) golden syrup or treacle
- 600 g (1 lb 5 oz) grated carrot (approximately 7 carrots)
- 120 g (4¼ oz) chopped walnuts

EQUIPMENT
- pencil
- good-quality baking paper
- two 18 cm (7 inch) cake tins
- two 20 cm (8 inch) cake tins
- scissors
- electric kitchen scales
- measuring spoons and cups
- sieve
- 2 large mixing bowls
- 2 jugs or medium mixing bowls
- stand mixer with whisk attachment
- coarse grater for carrots
- silicone spatula
- metal spatula
- 2 wire racks
- 2 cake boards: 18 cm (7 inch) and 20 cm (8 inch)
- fine zester for lemon
- sharp knife
- piping (icing) bag with round large piping tip size 1A
- serrated knife or cake leveller

NOTE I suggest cooking the two smaller cakes (Batter A) in the oven followed by the two larger cakes (Batter B), rather than trying to fit everything into the oven at once. You can still prepare most of your ingredients at the same time by measuring, sifting and mixing the liquids together; just wait until right before baking to combine the wet and dry ingredients.

METHOD

1. Preheat the oven to 160°C (325°F) (FF).

2. Using your pencil, baking paper and cake tins, trace out two circles for each tin size, and cut them out. Also cut out four thick, long strips of baking paper for the sides of the tins.

3. Spray the tins lightly with canola oil, then line the tins with the baking paper circles and strips.

4. Weigh out all of the ingredients for your cakes but keep Batter A separate from Batter B. Sift all of the dry ingredients except the brown sugar into two large mixing bowls, one for each batter, and make a small well in the middle of each one.

5. Combine the sugar, eggs, olive oil and golden syrup for each batter in two jugs or medium-sized bowls, one for each cake size. Set aside the bowl for Batter B, as you won't mix that until your smaller cakes are out of the oven.

6. Using a stand mixer, slowly beat the liquid ingredients for Batter A into the dry ingredients for that cake, until everything is incorporated, then add the grated carrot and walnuts. Mix again for 1 minute until combined. Reminder: repeat this step for Batter B after you have finished baking the smaller cakes.

7. Divide Batter A between the two smaller cake tins — place the lined tins on the electric scale, zero out then weigh 900 g (2 lb) of the mixture into each tin, and smooth out with metal spatula in a clockwise direction. (When your cakes have been baked they will weigh less, about 850 g/ 1 lb 14 oz each.)

8. Bake the cakes for about 50 minutes. After that time, insert a skewer at an angle into the centre of each cake to see if it comes out clean. If not, bake for a few minutes more.

9. Allow the cakes to cool in their tins for 10 minutes before removing them to wire racks to cool completely.

10. Repeat steps 6 to 9 for the larger cakes, noting that each tin should have 1150 g (about 2 lb 7 oz) of batter added to it, and will need 55–60 minutes in the oven before testing.

11. When all the cakes have completely cooled, use a serrated knife or cake leveller to remove the top of each cake, so they are all nice and flat. After this, carefully cut the two larger cakes in half, horizontally, so you end up with four 20 cm (8 inch) layers.

FILLING AND ICING THE CAKE
LEMON CREAM CHEESE FILLING

INGREDIENTS
- 1.3 kg (3 lb) soft icing mixture or icing (confectioners') sugar
- 200 g (7 oz) unsalted butter, softened
- 500 g (1 lb 2 oz) cream cheese at room temperature
- finely grated zest and juice of 1 lemon
- 3 teaspoons vanilla extract or essence
- 32 small sugar roses with a little red petal dust on them (optional), to finish the cake

METHOD

1. Sift the soft icing mixture into the bowl of a stand mixer with a whisk attachment.

2. Add the softened butter and cream cheese to the bowl.

3. On a slow speed, begin to whisk the ingredients together.

4. Add the lemon zest and juice, and the vanilla extract.

5. Increase the speed to high once all the ingredients have started to combine, and beat for about 5 minutes. The icing mixture should be smooth and fluffy, but slightly thick. You don't want your mixture to be runny at all.

TIP To avoid your icing becoming runny, start by adding the liquids — the lemon juice, for example, very slowly. If you find that your icing is quite wet and runny, you can add extra sugar slowly until it has reached a thick and fluffy consistency.

6. Place the lemon filling in a piping (icing) bag fitted with a pipe tip.

7. Pipe a small dot in the centre of your 20 cm (8 inch) cake board, then add the first 20 cm (8 inch) cake layer to the board, ensuring the baked side faces down.

8. From the centre of the cake, using a clockwise motion, pipe the filling so it looks like a spiral when you are finished (see page 160). Add the next layer, baked side down, and repeat until you have piped three layers of filling. The last layer should not have any piped icing over it.

9. Add a heaped tablespoon of lemon icing to the centre of the top layer and, using a spatula, smooth it out.

10. Pipe a small dot of the icing in the centre of the 18 cm (7 inch) cake board then gently place one of the smaller cakes, baked side down on the board. Press down gently to secure in place. The 18 cm (7 inch) cake does not have any cut layers, so you'll only have to pipe the icing one more time.

NOTE When icing and layering your cakes, reserve the layers that have one side baked for the bottom layer and flip the top cake upside down, so you have a smooth area to decorate on.

11. Pipe the icing, as before, then place the last cake on top, baked side facing up this time.

12. Spoon a heaped tablespoon of icing on top and smooth, out with spatula.

13. Any leftover icing you have can be used to smear and smooth around the side of the two cakes. The two levels should look like they have a faint coating of icing.

14. Place the layered cakes in the fridge to allow the cream cheese icing to cool and set. This should take about 1 hour. If you can leave them for 4 hours, even better.

15. Once the cakes have chilled sufficiently, you are ready to start decorating with the buttercream.

BUTTERCREAM ICING

METHOD

Make a double batch of the basic buttercream (p. 68) and add 2 small drops of AmeriColor Soft Gel Paste in Red Red.

DECORATING THE CAKE

METHOD

1. To decorate, the same principles apply as on page 161 (re-read that page before you start, to get you in the zone): you want to start with the larger cake first, preferably on a cake turntable so you can easily apply the buttercream and rotate your cake with spatula in hand.

2. Apply a heaped spatula of buttercream at a time, smearing it evenly all around the cake before adding the next lot, ensuring it is even around the cake. It does not need to be perfectly smooth, just a nice even spread of buttercream.

3. When you have finished covering the side and the top of the cake with buttercream, add a small amount of buttercream to your spatula and, starting from the top edge of your cake with your hand slightly tilted down, smear the buttercream downwards. This will create a small diagonal wave-like appearance.

4. Continue doing this all around the cake.

5. Repeat steps 2 to 4 with the smaller cake.

6. Gently place a clean 18 cm (7 inch) cake tin on the centre of the top of the 20 cm (8 inch) cake to make a mark on the surface. This will help you to correctly place the smaller cake on the larger one (see page 207).

7. Place the smaller tier on the larger one, with your hands holding the cake board on either side (don't panic if you drop it a little hard), and use a spatula to lift and push it into the centre if you missed the mark.

8. Add little sugar roses around the cake for the finishing touch, if you like.

FLAMINGO SPIRIT

This is a simple three-layer chocolate cake made using a **triple batch of the Batter B** on page 190. Bake and cool the cakes, then chill in the fridge for at least an hour while you make a double batch of **chocolate ganache** (p. 113). Fill the layers of cake with one of the batches of ganache (see the technique on page 160). Spread a layer of buttercream (p. 68) all over the cake, smooth it out, then return the cake to the fridge for an at least an hour to chill. Decorate with warmed ganache following the technique on page 214. Finish with 16 **pink macaron shells** (p. 108), some **pink sprinkles**, **clear sugar sand** and a **flamingo candle**.

SMOOTHING AND GANACHING

1

2

3

4

5

6

Remove the chilled cake from the fridge and place carefully on a cake-decorating turntable. If you don't have one, place the cake on a board or a tray and just turn that as you go.

1–2 Wet a clean cloth very slightly so it is damp, and run it gently around the cake to smooth it out.

3 Use a cake scraper to smooth around the edges and the top, dragging it gently inwards on top.

4 Gently warm a batch of ganache (p. 113) in a microwave, or in a heatproof bowl placed over a saucepan of simmering water. Pour the melted ganache into a jug, and while it's a pourable consistency, start to pour over the cold cake in a slow steady stream so it pools on the top of the cake. Either leave as a drip cake or smooth out the chocolate.

5 Use a metal spatula to smooth out the ganache. Repeat until the cake is completely covered.

6 Chill the cake in the fridge for 15 minutes, then add more ganache and use an offset spatula to create waves, if you like. Throw sprinkles at the cake so they stick to the sides then top with macaron shells (p. 108) and a fun candle to finish off the look.

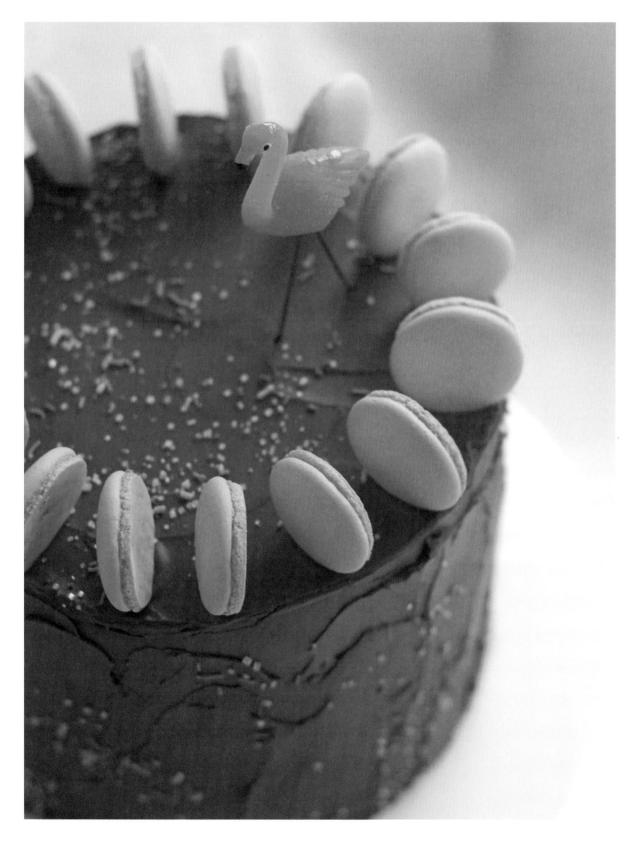

This cake is a fun, modern take on my celebration cakes. Inspired by my love for painting, this design celebrates abstract art and colour. I used the Orange Bloom cake (p. 198) and then decorated it as opposite.

PAINTED CAKE

Learning to paint freestyle will add a new dimension to your cake decorating.

1 Reserve a few tablespoons of the buttercream used for filling the cakes. Once the cakes are stacked, apply a basic crumb coat of buttercream (p. 160) and chill in the fridge for at least 1 hour.

2 Make a batch of white frosting (p. 204) then apply it to the cake, using the roughly iced technique (p. 177).

3 Divide the reserved buttercream into three or four, depending on how many colours you want to 'paint' on the cake. Add a drop of colour to each buttercream. You don't need lots of colours — just a touch of black can make a big difference. I've used four colours here: Peach, Fuschia, Electric Pink and Black.

4 Using a food-only paint brush or pastry brush, apply one colour to the cake at a time, smearing it one direction. Continue until you feel you have enough of that particular colour around the cake. Repeat the process with the next colour.

5 Pipe finishing touches using the colours of buttercream, if you like.

Layer nine

WAFFLE JOURNEY

Each day holds a lesson you can learn from.
Build your knowledge, then apply it.

in Layer nine ...

MORNING, SUNSHINE

My husband and I used to disagree about waffles:
he liked pancakes, I preferred waffles. So we ate pancakes.

But once the kids started asking for waffles too, a Sunday tradition
was born. They really are the perfect morning breakfast/brunch item,
because you can make them into your own style and creation.

One of the best things about waffles is that even though they're
so easy to make, they can be plated up and transformed into
something beautiful. And because the waffle itself isn't overly sweet
or strong in flavour, the combinations of ingredients you can
play with for their toppings are endless.

I love their sharp, strong lines, and when you add brightly
coloured fruits, a drizzle of pretty syrup or a few edible flowers,
the humble breakfast waffle becomes another creature: an
elegant and delicious dessert, easy to devour any time of day.

BASIC WAFFLES

MAKES: 6 waffles

PREP TIME: 10 minutes   COOKING TIME: 18 minutes.

INGREDIENTS
- 75 g (2¾ oz) butter, melted
- 200 g (7 oz) self-raising flour
- 1 egg
- 1 teaspoon salt
- 2 teaspoons vanilla extract or essence
- 280 ml (10 fl oz) milk
- canola oil cooking spray

EQUIPMENT
- measuring jug
- measuring spoons
- small saucepan
- whisk
- electric kitchen scales
- large mixing bowl
- waffle iron

METHOD
1. Preheat the oven to 100°C (200°F) fan-forced (FF).

2. Place the melted butter and 2 tablespoons of the flour in a large bowl. Whisk until the ingredients resemble a thick paste, similar to a roux.

3. Add the egg and whisk until combined.

4. Add the salt, vanilla extract and milk, and whisk until the mixture is incorporated. It should look runny and wet at this stage.

5. Gradually add the remaining flour and continue to whisk until the mixture forms a thick batter.

6. Lightly spray the waffle iron with canola oil, and then turn it to a medium heat — you want the iron moderately hot but not burning.

7. Add a ladleful of the batter to the iron, but don't completely fill it otherwise the batter will overflow when you close it.

8. Cook each side for about 2 minutes or until golden brown, then move to a tray and place in the oven to keep warm while you cook the rest of the waffles.

9. Waffles get a lovely crispness when kept warm in the oven. If you don't have your decorating ingredients ready, reduce the oven temperature to 60°C (140°F) (FF) and then increase it to 100°C (200°F) (FF) for 5 minutes just before you are ready to decorate and serve.

FILLING YOUR WAFFLE MAKER

Tip
Use a small pouring jug to measure out each waffle if a ladle is too messy or difficult. Use a metal offset spatula to smear the batter evenly around the maker.

1

2

3

4

5

6

*Spiced apple waffles are a delicious and
pretty breakfast or dessert*

THREE WAFFLE TOPPINGS

SPICED APPLE WAFFLES

MAKES: **6 waffles**

INGREDIENTS
- maple syrup
- 1 batch of spiced apple (p. 231)
- 400 ml (14 fl oz) thickened (whipping) cream, whipped
- snow sugar

METHOD
1. How you style these will depend on how you like to serve your waffles, and how many you want to eat. For individual servings, put a waffle on each plate, drizzle over some maple syrup, follow with a few slices of spiced apple and a dollop of whipped cream. Sift some snow sugar over each plate to finish.

2. For a more dramatic look, pile up the waffles on a nice serving plate, follow the same steps as above but sift the snow sugar at the table, in front of your guests. Bring the remaining whipped cream, maple syrup and spiced apples to the table for your guests to add to their own plates.

#WAFFLELOVE

MAKES: **6 waffles**

NOTE If you have a heart-shaped waffle iron, you will be able to divide each waffle into 4 smaller hearts and serve 4 hearts per person.

METHOD
1. Melt 40 g (1½ oz) of dark chocolate (70% cocoa) in a microwave in short bursts then dip a teaspoon into the chocolate and wave your hand across the cooked waffles to create thin chocolate lines.

2. Decorate with a large punnet of hulled and halved strawberries.

3. If you like ice cream with your waffles (and who doesn't?), add a scoop of vanilla × rhubarb ice cream (p. 124). Serve on a large platter.

PEANUT BUTTER WAFFLE LOVE

MAKES: **6 waffles**

INGREDIENTS
- peanut butter ice cream (p. 124)
- 2 bananas, thinly sliced
- maple syrup
- 2 handfuls of macadamia nuts, roughly chopped

METHOD
1. Top each waffle with a scoop of peanut butter ice cream. Arrange a few slices of banana off to the side of the ice cream.

2. Drizzle a little maple syrup over each waffle before adding a few macadamia nuts to each serving.

#wafflelove

peanut butter waffle love

Pretty pinks
and purples

Styling with toppings

A really easy but pretty way to serve waffles is to decorate them with fresh fruit, a dusting of snow sugar, pinches of Persian fairy floss (similar to fairy floss/cotton candy) and some edible flowers. If you're having a large group of family or friends over, stick to three different design styles. Here, I've used a square double-waffle iron using the basic waffle recipe on page 222. I've topped the golden waffles off with the three flavour combinations below, then finished each one off with a drizzle of maple syrup.

Fresh figs and blueberries with snow sugar
Strawberries and rosewater Persian fairy floss
Mixed fresh or frozen berries with edible flowers

SPICED APPLE AND EASY SYRUPS

These apples and fruit syrups are a perfect (and pretty) addition to waffles but can also be drizzled over desserts such as pavlova and cupcakes, and used in cocktails for a touch of colour and flavour. Each of these syrups keeps for 3 days in the fridge and makes about 50 ml (1½ fl oz) — enough to drizzle over 6 waffles. Double the recipe if you want to make enough to drizzle over porridge the next morning, or pavlovas (p. 58).

SPICED APPLE

INGREDIENTS
- 1 pink lady apple, thinly sliced (a mandoline is best for this)
- 1½ tablespoons caster (superfine) sugar
- 3 tablespoons water
- ½ teaspoon ground cinnamon
- juice of ½ a lemon

METHOD
Place all the ingredients in a small heavy-based saucepan and bring to the boil, then reduce the heat and simmer for 5 minutes. Remove from the heat and place the apple slices in an airtight container with a drizzle of their syrup to cool down before serving. Alternatively, store the container in the fridge for up to 3 days.

SUGARED APPLE OR MANDARIN SYRUP

INGREDIENTS
- 100 ml (3½ fl oz) water
- 4 strawberries, hulled and halved
- ½ a pink lady apple, thinly sliced (a mandoline is best for this), or 1 mandarin, unpeeled and washed well
- 100 g (3½ oz) caster (superfine) sugar
- juice of ½ a lemon

METHOD
Place all the ingredients in a heavy-based saucepan and bring to the boil. Cook for 7–10 minutes, or until the syrup is slightly thick. Remove from the heat and allow to cool completely before transferring to an airtight container. If using mandarin, strain through a fine sieve and discard the mandarin pulp. Keep in the fridge until ready to use.

STICKY ORANGE SYRUP

INGREDIENTS

- 100 ml (3½ fl oz) water
- 2 strawberries, hulled and cut in half
- ½ a navel orange, thinly sliced (leave peel on and remove the seeds)
- 100 g (3½ oz) caster (superfine) sugar
- juice of ½ a lemon

METHOD

Place all the ingredients in a small heavy-based saucepan, and bring to the boil. Cook for 10–15 minutes, or until the syrup is slightly thick. Remove from the heat and allow to cool completely before transferring the syrup and the fruit to an airtight container. Keep in the fridge until ready to use.

PRETTY-IN-PINK RHUBARB SYRUP

INGREDIENTS

- 100 ml (3½ fl oz) water
- 250 g (9 oz) chopped rhubarb
- ½ a white peach, thinly sliced (optional)
- 100 g (3½ oz) caster (superfine) sugar
- juice of ½ a lemon

METHOD

Place all the ingredients in a medium heavy-based saucepan, and bring to the boil. Cook for 10–15 minutes, or until the syrup is slightly thick. Carefully strain the syrup through a sieve into an airtight container, and discard the fruit. Allow the syrup to cool down before placing a lid on top. Keep in the fridge until ready to use.

NOTE If you want to keep the rhubarb pieces in your syrup, keep an eye on the rhubarb and poke it with a fork every few minutes. Once tender, remove it from the pan. Strain the syrup, as above, then return the pieces to the syrup before storing.

SIMPLE BLUEBERRY SYRUP

INGREDIENTS

- 1 × 400 g (14 oz) tin of blueberries in syrup
- 250 g (9 oz) caster (superfine) sugar

METHOD

1. Place both ingredients in a medium heavy-based saucepan and bring to the boil. Once boiling, reduce the heat to medium–low and simmer for 30 minutes, stirring occasionally, until the syrup starts to thicken.

2. Remove from the heat and transfer to a heatproof container to cool completely. The syrup will continue to thicken as it cools. Use straight away or keep in the fridge in an airtight container until ready to use. Serve warm, spooned over the waffles, and top with pretty little edible flowers.

BLUEBERRY WAFFLE HAZE

Great comfort comes from eating **warm waffles** (p. 222) with generous drizzles of **blueberry syrup** (opposite). A few **frozen berries** sprinkled on top and slowly defrosting into the hot waffles will provide a refreshing and exciting contrast at the start of a hot summer's day. Warm crispy waffles, cold berries and juicy syrup ... a balanced and harmonious way to greet the morning.

Layer ten

COCKTAIL JOURNEY

*Wildflowers, with their different shapes, heights
and colours, work so well together in a landscape.
Apply this principle to your drinks by mixing decorative
straws, fruits, edible flowers, coloured ice cubes,
and different sizes and shapes of serving glasses.*

in Layer ten ...

TOAST YOUR SUCCESS

A pretty cocktail is the perfect accompaniment to a dessert, and it doesn't have be complicated either. Beautiful glasses or an array of drinks in pretty colours make a great statement and are a brilliant way of breaking the ice at an event. Simple ingredients like fruit syrups, fruits, herbs and good-quality store-bought juices in interesting flavour combinations can help you add that extra something when you're short on time.

INFUSION & SPIRITS

Infusing is a great way of adding additional depth and flavour to your cocktails. It's a simple technique where fruit, peels and/or spices and/or herbs sit in the alcohol for a period of time so their flavours marry together. Fruit only needs a couple of hours, whereas fruit peels can stay in the alcohol for a week. Spirits like vodka and gin take on infusions really well. There really aren't any rules; mix and match flavours you like and see where it takes you.

SUGGESTED FLAVOUR PAIRINGS:
- gin: lemon and/or lime peel with ½ a bunch of mint
- vodka: 1 punnet of strawberries or a few fresh chillies, pricked

FLAVOUR OPTIONS
- citrus: lemon, lime, orange or mandarin peel
- herbs: rosemary, fresh mint or coriander
- spices: cloves, cinnamon, star anise or coriander seeds
- fruits and other interesting flavours: strawberries, chillies (pricked), tea leaves

STRAWBERRY-INFUSED GIN × TONIC

MAKES: 1 drink

INGREDIENTS
- 50 ml (1½ fl oz) gin
- 150 ml (5 fl oz) tonic water
- 5 strawberries, hulled

METHOD

1. Halve 3 of the strawberries and let them steep in the gin for a couple of hours.

2. Remove and discard the strawberries. Either transfer the infused gin to an airtight bottle to drink later, or pour into a glass. Add some ice and tonic water, then halve the remaining strawberries and add them to the glass for a pretty garnish.

PINK SPARKLE

Fill three-quarters of a champagne flute or small glass with **pink lemonade**. Top up with your favourite **Champagne** (or non-alcoholic sparkling drink) then garnish each glass with 4 **fresh raspberries**. If planning a party, this is a really easy cocktail to prepare ahead of time. Just add the Champagne and raspberries right as your guests arrive. (MAKES ONE 125 ML/4 FL OZ DRINK)

WATERMELON REFRESHER

Cut up a few slices of **watermelon**, remove the rind and any seeds, then run the fruit through a juicer. Pass the watermelon juice through a fine sieve and then through muslin (cheesecloth) so it's really clean and clear. You may need to do this a few times. Pour the juice into your favourite glass, add 50 ml (1¾ fl oz) **watermelon vodka** per glass (optional), some **ice** and a few **frozen berries**. Garnish with a small sprig of **mint** and enjoy. (MAKES ONE 200 ML/7 FL OZ DRINK)

JUICING FLAVOURS

Using an electric juicer means it is quick to make your own favourite flavoured drinks. Lots of ice, and some small, pretty garnishes can transform any occasion.

LYCHEE & APPLE
- 1 × 400 g (14 oz) tin of lychees in juice
- 1 pink lady apple

CARROT, ORANGE & GINGER
- 1 carrot
- 1 thumb-sized piece of fresh ginger
- 2 oranges, peeled

BERRY & KIWI
- 250 g (9 oz) strawberries, hulled
- 6 raspberries
- ½ a kiwi fruit, peeled

WATERMELON, STRAWBERRY & BEETROOT
- 3 slices of watermelon, peeled and seeds removed
- 4 strawberries, hulled
- 1 beetroot (beet), washed and trimmed

ORANGE & STRAWBERRY
- 3 oranges, peeled
- 4 strawberries, hulled

WATERMELON, APPLE & GINGER
- 2–3 thick slices of watermelon, peeled and seeds removed
- 1 pink lady apple
- 1 thumb-sized piece of fresh ginger

ADDITIONAL FLAVOURS
- mint with orange and lime
- passionfruit with blood orange
- frozen or fresh blackberries with mandarins

PRETTY GARNISHES
- blueberries on small cocktail skewers
- lemons and/or limes: thinly sliced or strips of zest
- lemons: sliced, wedged, strips of zest or rind (without the bitter pith)
- thinly sliced peaches with a drop of rosewater
- vanilla bean pods
- small sprigs of rosemary

ORANGE × CARROT
RUM TWIST

Using a juicer, juice 4 **oranges**, 2 **carrots** and a thumb-sized piece of **fresh ginger**. Strain the juice through a sieve and then pass it through muslin (cheesecloth), to ensure the juice is clean and clear. You may need to do this a couple of times. Pour into your favourite glass then add 50 ml (1¾ fl oz) **white rum** per glass (optional), **ice** and a half a slice of **orange** to garnish.
(MAKES ONE 200 ML/7 FL OZ DRINK)

PINK TEQUILA

MAKES: *4–6 drinks*

INGREDIENTS
- 1 litre (35 fl oz/4 cups) sparkling pink apple or pink grapefruit juice
- 50 ml (1½ fl oz) tequila per glass
- ice
- lime slices, to garnish

METHOD

1. Fill each glass with a good amount of sparkling juice.

2. Add tequila to each glass.

3. Fill each glass with a small handful of ice, then garnish with a slice of lime.

TIP Tall glasses are perfect for serving this drink, especially with gold straws.

LYCHEE SQUEEZE

Hull 8 large **strawberries**. Slice 2 of them. Use a juicer, blender or food processor to purée 400 g (14 oz) **tinned lychees in juice** – juice and all – with the remaining strawberries. Strain the juice through a fine sieve and then again through muslin (cheesecloth) to ensure the juice is really clean and clear. You may need to do this a couple of times. Pour into your glass. Top with a splash of **sparkling mineral water** and a few strawberry slices, and serve. (MAKES ONE 200 ML/ 7 FL OZ DRINK)

LEMON LIME BITTERS

Fill each glass with **sparking lemon lime bitters** (you'll need about 250 ml/ 9 fl oz per glass) and add **ice**, if you like. Dip a straw into a bottle of any juice that has **beetroot (beet)** in it, place your finger on top of the straw to trap the juice and then let your finger go to drop it into the glass of bitters. Beautiful pink smoke will swirl around the glass before settling. It's nice theatre when you have guests over. Repeat for each glass and garnish with an **edible flower**, if you like. (MAKES FOUR 250 ML/9 FL OZ DRINKS)

APPLE STAR TEASER

MAKES: 6

INGREDIENTS
- 1 litre (35 fl oz/4 cups) cold-pressed apple juice with raspberry (see note)
- 750 ml (26 fl oz/3 cups) sparking mineral water, to top up the glasses
- 1 pink lady apple
- gold leaf

METHOD

1. Fill three-quarters of each glass with the apple and raspberry juice.

2. Top the glasses up with the sparkling mineral water.

3. Slice the apple into thin slices then use a star-shaped cookie cutter to cut out thin pink lady apple stars for decoration.

4. For something super special, add some gold leaf detail to the rim of the each glass. If you don't have gold leaf, you can gently rim the glass with some white sugar sand before making the cocktail.

NOTE You should be able to find this blend of juice, or similar, in good supermarkets and boutique grocers. If you can't find any interesting blends, use regular apple juice instead.

Layer eleven

POPSICLE JOURNEY

The colours in her eyes danced
in the sunlight

in Layer eleven ...

FROZEN BEAUTIES

These popsicles are all made from store-bought juices and sparkling drinks. They're perfect solutions when you're running out of time for an event but still want to create something pretty and fun.

If you don't have a juicer, these are also a good alternative but if you do have a juicer, you can make any flavour of juice that suits your taste and freeze it.

Popiscles are so easy and fun to make when the warmer weather kicks in. You can easily cater to different tastes as well, thanks to the individual moulds — perfect for fussy guests! I love the colours I'm able to introduce simply by using different juices and ingredients. They look incredible when served together on a platter, which is also a really nice way to serve something simple, but in a way that feels special and slightly unusual.

Use any of the recipes from the cocktails layer (p. 234) for your popsicles. They're super fun and pretty, especially when served together. Perfect for spring and summer events.

BLUEBERRY DREAMER

Put 400 ml (14 fl oz) of **milk** (non-dairy milk will also work) in a blender with a punnet of **fresh blueberries**, ½ a handful of **frozen blueberries**, and 2 scoops of **vanilla ice cream** or 160 g (5¾ oz) of **plain yoghurt**. Blend until it has a smoothie consistency then divide between your popsicle moulds and freeze according to the manufacturer's instructions. **TIP** For two-tone popsicles, make half a batch with one berry, and half a batch with another. Semi-fill the moulds with one flavour, freeze, and then top with the other before freezing again. (MAKES 8)

SPARKLING APPLE/GUAVA ×
ROSEWATER POPSICLES

For these pretty popsicles, mix 650 ml (22½ fl oz) **sparkling mineral water** with 150 ml (5 fl oz) **apple (or guava) cordial** and 1½ teaspoons of **rosewater** in a large jug. After stirring well, divide between popsicle moulds (follow the manufacturer's instructions). Place in the freezer overnight to set. To serve, spread a layer of ice on a platter, arrange some pretty flowers around the side, then place the popsicles in the middle. These are perfect for a spring or summer event. (MAKES 8)

HIBISCUS TEA POPSICLES

MAKES: 8–10 popsicles

INGREDIENTS
- 2 tablespoons hibiscus tea leaves
- 800 ml (28 fl oz) boiling water
- 2 tablespoons caster (superfine) sugar
- 1 navel orange, thinly sliced
- 7 strawberries, hulled
- 8 mint leaves (optional)

METHOD
1. Brew the hibiscus tea using a teapot with an infuser. If you don't have a teapot, place the tea leaves in a fine sieve over a heatproof jug. Add the sugar to the water and allow to steep for 5 minutes before removing all of the tea leaves.

2. Add 4 thin orange slices and 5 halved strawberries to the tea, then leave for half an hour to infuse and cool down to room temperature.

3. Remove the fruit from the cooled tea and pour the tea into the popsicle moulds. Thinly slice the 2 remaining strawberries. Quarter 4 thin slices of orange. Divide the additional slices of fruit and some small mint leaves, if using, between the popsicles.

4. Put the lid on and insert the sticks into the popsicles (according to manufacturer's instructions) then place in the freezer and leave overnight.

RED POPSICLE LOVER

MAKES: *8 popsicles*

INGREDIENTS
- ¼ of a watermelon, rind and seeds removed
- 5 strawberries, hulled
- 1 small beetroot (beet), washed and trimmed
- 1 teaspoon pear essence
- 200–300 ml (7–10½ fl oz) sparkling mineral water

METHOD
1. Juice the watermelon, strawberries and beetroot.

2. Strain the juice through a sieve and then pass it through muslin (cheesecloth), to remove any pulp. You should get at least 400–500 ml (14–17 fl oz/about 2 cups) of juice, but the exact amount will depend on how much liquid the juicer extracts, and how big and/or juicy your fruit is.

3. Add the pear essence, then the sparkling mineral water, and divide between your popsicle moulds. Top up with sparkling water, if needed. Put the lid on and insert the sticks into the popsicles (according to manufacturer's instructions), then place in the freezer and leave overnight.

4. Spread some frozen berries on a chilled platter then put the popsicles on top and serve to your guests.

INDEX

*These are the places I use for my equipment,
props and general party supplies*

CAKE & COOKWARE
- KitchenAid Australia
- The Essential Ingredient
- West's Cakes Decoration
- Blackwood Lane
- Riess Cookware
- Wilton
- Normann Copenhagen
- Wheel & Barrow

PARTY SUPPLIES
- Glistening Occasions
- Poppies for Grace

FLOWERS
- Cartel Flowers
- Flower in a Box

PAINTS
- Taubmans

ART AND PAPER SUPPLIES
- The Paper Place

HOMEWARE AND LIVING
- West Elm Australia
- Williams-Sonoma Australia
- Robert Gordon Australia
- Ikea Australia
- Provincial Home Living
- Neue Blvd
- AURA Home
- Dowel Jones
- Resident GP Homewares & Gifts
- Lavallier Emporium
- Waterford Crystal
- Kikki K
- Domayne Australia
- Norsu Interiors
- Bluebellgray
- Royal Albert

THANKS TO ...

Dreams do come true ...

A lover and collector of beautiful books, in my wildest dreams I did not think I'd ever be able to share my work, ideas and inspiration with you in a book. I remember saying to my mother one year into starting Nectar and Stone, 'Imagine if I could write a book.' And my mother said, 'Now that is a wonderful dream to have.' She didn't say it meaning that it was impossible, or that she didn't believe in me, but neither of us knew what wonderful things were ahead for Nectar and Stone.

I've been so blessed and fortunate to have been surrounded by amazing and talented people who I want to share with you because they helped make this journey and book possible.

I start with my husband, Nicholas. You provided me with the freedom to explore and develop. You funded, believed, supported and pushed me to be the best I could. Without you I don't think Nectar and Stone would have been. You energised and motivated me to start believing in my creativity, and you nurtured and supported me emotionally when I thought things were impossible.

My sons — Isaiah and Dimitri — you were the building blocks to starting my business. Isaiah's fussy eating habits brought out my creativity, and Dimitri's neck problems from birth, which required all my focus and energy to get him recovered (thankfully fully fixed now), instilled in me this dark frustration which started to be released and resolved through my dessert design.

My mother, Maria, my backbone. You are a saint and treasure, always there for me, pushing me to make my dreams a reality. You raised me to always being open to learning, sharing and work hard. You empowered me to believe in myself and my capabilities. Your love for family being together at the heart of the table, especially around celebrations, has had such an impact on me and is certainly a tradition that I want to carry on.

My father, Dimitrios, my freedom. You encouraged me to stay home and raise my kids. You said you would support me if needed. 'Enjoy your kids and see them grow.' This type of support is freedom. I'm grateful that you made me feel so secure.

My sisters — Mishel, Toula and Filisaty — your constant support, love and motivation has been so appreciated. I'm so lucky to have you in my life. And to my in-laws Chris and Del, thank you from the bottom of my heart for always being available, supportive and for your words of encouragement.

Women empower women. To the amazing Diana Hill, my publisher at Murdoch Books, for seeking me out with this incredible opportunity and believing that I could do it. You are such an inspiring lady — I'm so humbled that you had the confidence and vision in me to create this. And to the beautiful team: Katie Bosher, Madeleine Kane and Vivien Valk — immersing yourself in my world, travelling along my footsteps and capturing the spirit, heart and soul of this book. From crafting my words to helping consolidate and express my emotions, to designing and laying out my images, this is the essence of me — and was such a beautiful collaboration of women working together, I loved every second of it.

Lastly, my community and beautiful clients. You provided me with opportunities, self-belief, self-love, motivation and interaction. I wake up every day so passionate and in love with what I do, but I know that this was, and is, made possible because of you. Through you I have grown, developed, evolved and changed as a woman, all for the better. I hope that this book makes you proud, is part of your home and journey — is something for you to cherish as you are part of this journey and captured in this book.

Caz xox

Published in 2017 by Murdoch Books, an imprint of Allen & Unwin

Murdoch Books Australia
83 Alexander Street
Crows Nest NSW 2065
Phone: +61 (0) 2 8425 0100
Fax: +61 (0) 2 9906 2218
murdochbooks.com.au
info@murdochbooks.com.au

Murdoch Books UK
Ormond House
26–27 Boswell Street
London WC1N 3JZ
Phone: +44 (0) 20 8785 5995
murdochbooks.co.uk
info@murdochbooks.co.uk

For Corporate Orders & Custom Publishing, contact our Business Development
Team at salesenquiries@murdochbooks.com.au.

Publisher: Diana Hill
Editorial Manager: Katie Bosher
Design Manager: Madeleine Kane
Designer: Vivien Valk
Photography, styling and recipe development: Caroline Khoo
Production Manager: Rachel Walsh

A cataloguing-in-publication entry is available from the catalogue of
the National Library of Australia at nla.gov.au.

ISBN 978 1 74336 882 4 Australia
ISBN 978 1 74336 887 9 UK

A catalogue record for this book is available from the British Library.

Colour reproduction by Splitting Image Colour Studio Pty Ltd, Clayton, Victoria
Printed by 1010 Printing International Limited, China
Reprinted 2017(Twice)

IMPORTANT: Those who might be at risk from the effects of salmonella
poisoning (the elderly, pregnant women, young children and those suffering
from immune deficiency diseases) should consult their doctor with any
concerns about eating raw eggs.

OVEN GUIDE: You may find cooking times vary depending on the oven you
are using. Fan-forced temperatures have been used throughout this book.
If you don't have a fan-forced setting on your oven, set the oven temperature
20°C (70°F) higher than indicated in the recipe.

MEASURES GUIDE: We have used 20 ml (4 teaspoon) tablespoon measures.
If you are using a 15 ml (3 teaspoon) tablespoon add an extra teaspoon of
the ingredient for each tablespoon specified.